Reading, Writing, and Discussing at the Graduate Level

A Guidebook for International Students

Rina Kim, Lillie R. Albert, and Hang Gyun Sihn

University Press of America,® Inc.
Lanham • Boulder • New York • Toronto • Plymouth, UK

Copyright © 2014 by University Press of America,® Inc.
4501 Forbes Boulevard, Suite 200, Lanham, Maryland 20706
UPA Aquisitions Department (301) 459-3366

10 Thornbury Road, Plymouth PL6 7PP, United Kingdom

Library of Congress Control Number: 2014941190
ISBN: 978-0-7618-6412-7 (paperback   )—ISBN: 978-0-7618-6413-4 (electronic)

To our family and friends,

and to international graduate students everywhere

Contents

Preface

The purpose of this book is to help international graduate students navigate the academic issues they will encounter in the course of their studies. From our investigation of international graduate students, we found that the majority of these students struggle with performing academic work at the graduate level. The level of international students' English is not the only issue; rather, international students may not know or understand the academic expectations for them in the United States. These difficulties may also be caused by cultural differences between the United States and other countries. In considering cultural differences in the academic field, this book provides detailed guidelines and suggestions as to how international students can manage academic work and social relationships while attending graduate school in the United States.

The target audiences for this book are international students who are enrolled in graduate courses in the United States, and those who are preparing to enter graduate school. In particular, this book targets international graduate students who are proficient in English but lack experience in navigating and functioning academically in graduate school. We have written a book that offers practical and hands-on information about how to be successful in the academic environment. The information and issues addressed in the book are composed simply, so that international graduate students can use it without having someone deconstruct the information for them.

With the help of this book, international students may understand the expected level of academic work for graduate students in the United States. It covers the kinds of questions international graduate students often ask when they study or work in the United States. In particular, international students may find answers to the following questions:

- How can I develop my own ideas based on the readings required for the course?
- How do I participate in classroom discussions effectively?
- How do I organize academic papers?
- How may I present my ideas successfully during class?
- How can I develop good relationship with professors, instructors, and graduate students?

Although the target audience is international graduate students, we envision that professionals providing support to them will also benefit from this work. Those who administer offices of graduate admissions and student services will find this book useful when answering inquires from potential international graduate students regarding academic support offered by their institution. Also, this book is an excellent resource for professors and instructors, because it is written from the point of view of international graduate students. It provides insightful information about their experiences, while at the same time presenting constructive material for those instructing and mentoring them.

In order to comprise various perspectives from different cultures, this book is a collaborative effort among three authors who have different academic backgrounds and cultural experiences. The first author, Rina Kim, is a doctoral student at Boston College. As an international student, Kim draws from her own experiences and the difficulties she and other international graduate students have encountered in performing academic work. The second author, Lillie R. Albert, is an Associate Professor in the Lynch School of Education at Boston College. Albert has a long professional history of teaching and working in the field of international education, which includes experience in Russia, South Africa, and most recently, South Korea. Her research has been published in both national and international journals and books. The third author, Hang Gyun Sihn, is the president of Seoul National University of Education in South Korea. As a scholar with international perspectives, Sihn discusses academic expectations for graduate students.

Introduction

While working for several years with diverse international students, we found that the majority struggled with graduate-level work because they neither knew nor understood the academic expectations for graduate students in the United States. The international students we met were fluent in English, and we had no problem interacting with them. The majority of international students we met reported that they merely sit in their classes without participating in discussions.

One of the international students explained, "I do understand what the professor and students talk about. However, whenever I tried to participate, I felt like I was isolated and disconnected, although I do not have any issues with speaking in English. The U.S. students seemed not to understand what I wanted to say, and I could not find what the problems were. Therefore, I decided to sit quietly during the lesson."

Many other international students said they had difficulties with course readings. They explained that they had trouble developing their own ideas or critiques based on the required readings, although they understood them. As a result, we believe the level of English is not the problem international students face; rather, it is a matter of understanding academic culture and norms in the United States.

In this book, we provide detailed guidelines and suggestions to help international students manage academic work and social relationships while attending graduate school in the United States. We explain the academic and cultural differences between the United States and other countries in five chapters, each of which focuses on a major academic skill, such as reading, writing, and discussion. An overview of each chapter follows.

Chapter one explains the different purposes of readings at the graduate and undergraduate levels. By discussing typical readings assigned at the graduate level, this chapter offers practical tips on how to read the articles and prepare assignments.

Chapter two offers practical tips for participating in classroom discussions, including using starter sentences and developing grounds for arguments from course readings.

Chapter three outlines detailed explanations regarding internal and external rules for writing graduate-level papers. This chapter does not, however, cover general rules for good writing, such as grammar and sentence structure. Rather, this chapter focuses on writing papers at the graduate level when the primary aim is to develop a paper on the basis of a research question.

Chapter four describes ways students might prepare and lead in-class presentations. This chapter provides general guidance for classroom presentations rather than focusing on specific types of presentations. In particular, this chapter focuses on concrete tips for international students, including how to practice giving an oral presentation, how to work with group members, and how to engage the audience.

In chapter five, we discuss social etiquette to help international students build good relationships in the graduate school community. After having conversation with international students, we found that many struggled to develop relationships with professors and other students due to cultural differences.

Each chapter consists of several sections, and every section starts with a scenario that illustrates the difficulties international students face in that situation. We developed each scenario on informal conversations and interactions with international students and our own experiences. All names in the scenarios are pseudonyms. We also provide a detailed explanation of what instructors may expect from international students, and we offer practical, hands-on information about how to meet those academic expectations. The information in this book is delivered in a clear, straightforward style that is easy for international graduate students to understand and use entirely on their own.

Chapter One

Reading Scholarly Articles with Purpose

INTRODUCTION

International students should understand that there is a difference between the undergraduate and graduate levels in terms of the purpose of assigned readings. When you are an undergraduate student, you read a book in order to understand the concepts presented in that book. As a graduate student, however, you read a book in order to find implications for your own future studies. You need to know how to create new ideas by drawing on information from course readings. By presenting various types of readings assigned at the graduate level, this chapter offers practical tips about how to read articles for preparing assignments.

TYPES OF READINGS

Hwang: "For one of my courses, a professor required students to read one chapter from the book and to post questions about the reading before the class meets every week. But I did not know what questions I should ask about the reading. I understand clearly what the authors wrote. The thing is that I can't find any questions worth asking. The authors explained the concept very clearly in the book, which means . . . the authors already provided a clear description regarding my questions. So, there are no questions left after I finish reading the book. What should I post?"

In the United States, most courses require students to read several articles or chapters of a book before class. Some professors make use of a website

1

and require students to post their own ideas or questions on a discussion board before the lecture, while other professors expect students to participate directly in a classroom discussion.

Most international students with whom we have interacted believe that "the books or articles were published because they contained clear explanations of the concepts. I can't find any problems with the authors' ideas. Why should I have a question? Isn't it better for me to memorize the content in order to use it later?"

The conflict regarding readings is caused because professors and students may define the term *reading* quite differently. For professors, the course reading involves <u>critical analysis</u> of the text, whereas the students assume that reading involves <u>a process of understanding and memorizing.</u> Bloom's (1956) Taxonomy of Cognitive Objectives shows the difference clearly. (See Figure 1.1.)

Bloom's Taxonomy of Cognitive Objectives shows the hierarchy of intellectual attitudes and skills. At the graduate level, professors may require higher cognitive skills such as evaluating or creating when students read articles or books. You may hear professors say, "You need to read a book in a critical way." This indicates applying higher cognitive and metacognitive skills.

Yet for international students who have language barriers, it may not be easy to change reading strategies. For example, a challenge for students may involve trying to understand the content of the book because of unknown words or unfamiliar grammatical structure. In addition, the assumption is that you are a graduate student and have met the admissions requirements; there-

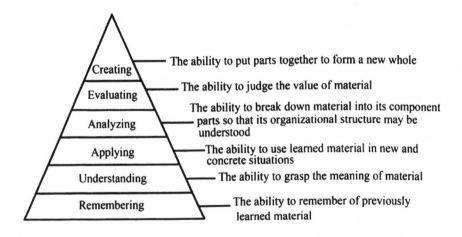

Figure 1.1.   Taxonomy of Cognitive Objectives.

fore, you are not provided with clear explanations about how to prepare for course readings.

Changing reading strategies does not occur overnight. Therefore, shifting strategies will require patience and practice. You may remember that when you were in middle or high school you learned how to summarize chapters in order to understand their major topic. These assignments gave you practice at reading for understanding or memorizing. Likewise, you need to practice reading with higher cognitive skills, although it may be a challenge for you.

A good strategy is to practice developing a set of questions before you start reading the text. These questions should require critical thinking, which goes beyond understanding and memorizing the material. The goal is not only to comprehend what is being communicated to you, but to interpret and make generalizations about the ideas presented. Answering the questions you constructed may help you develop a critical eye while reading. Examples of questions for each cognitive skill are as follows.

Creating

What are the implications of the findings?

How can I develop my own research based on the evaluation of the reading?

What are the connections among the articles that I have read for the course throughout the semester?

Evaluating

What are the strengths of the sample or case?

What are the limitations of the sample or case?

What are the strengths of the research method?

What are the limitations of the research method?

How do I judge the validity of the findings?

Analyzing

What is the nature of the sample or case?

How did the authors develop their argument?

Applying

How do the findings apply to my own situation?

How do the findings apply to my own country?

How can I apply the research method from the reading to my own study?

Understanding

What is the key argument this paper is making?
What research method is being used?

Remembering

What are the key factors I should remember?

It is not necessary for you to answer all of the questions. You may even create your own questions for each level of Bloom's Taxonomy. However, keeping these questions in mind when reading a book or journal article will help you overcome the urge to simply memorize information, because it will force you to focus on the other aspects of reading. The following examples show how to answer these questions when you read an article or a book.

1. [Understanding] What Is the Key Argument This Paper Is Making?

Although educational leaders must develop and articulate a much greater awareness of the ethical significance of their actions and decisions, discussions of ethics in education programs for educational leaders and in school practice are largely subjective and individually determined because of the pervasive contemporary climate of relativism.

Educational leaders should make an ethical decision by viewing an issue through a multi-dimensional lens, which includes conflicting perspectives on ethics, such as relativistic perspectives, rather than relying on personal beliefs or subjectivity.

The preparation programs for future school leaders should develop more comprehensive approaches to link ethical theory to practice in order to overcome relativistic uncertainty.

2. [Understanding] What Research Method Is Being Used?

The author supports her claim with a literature review. A literature review is an interpretation of previously published research by experts or researchers in a specific area of interest. The literature review may give the author an opportunity to look up former studies in order to find the strengths and weaknesses of the research.

3. [Applying] How Do the Findings Apply to My Own Situation?

The author provides a critical viewpoint toward the process of educational leaders' decision-making and current preparation programs for future school leaders by noting the contemporary climate of relativism. I also believe that the current decision-making process, which relies heavily on an individual leader's beliefs, is irresponsible. There needs to be a more systematic approach to support educational leaders' ethical decisions. As noted from the article, providing diverse perspectives may broaden educational leaders' understanding of problematic situations in the educational field. That is why educators, including principals and teachers, have a great need for education and experience. Before I came here, I was part of an elite group in South Korea. At that time, I could not understand students who had learning disabilities or who came from other countries. I could not make a proper educational decision for them because I did not understand their situations or problems. Since I came to the United States to study as an international student, I now understand students who come from neglected social groups. I experienced diverse problems because I was not "one of them" here and I did not know about classroom cultures and norms. Not only that, but I also learned diverse educational theories and perspectives from diverse courses. If I go back to my country and become an educational leader, I believe that I can make better decisions than before.

4. [Analyzing] What Is the Nature of the Sample or Case?

The author selected empirical studies as the sample of this study. Empirical study is a way of acquiring knowledge by means of observation or experience. Empirical data, which are collected based on research questions and methods, can be analyzed quantitatively or qualitatively.

5. [Evaluating] What Are the Strengths of the Sample or Case?

The strength of empirical studies is that the findings of the studies are generated from experimentation or observation. Therefore, empirical studies may help us understand and respond more appropriately to the dynamics of the situation. In addition, empirical studies provide insights into contextual differences.

6. [Evaluating] What Are the Limitations of the Sample or Case?

Although the author selects samples among empirical studies, most of the samples are qualitative studies. The purpose of a qualitative study is to understand a certain phenomenon rather than to generalize. The author conceives the problems of current preparation programs for future school leaders based on a literature review. However, the author references cases from qualitative studies, from which it may not be feasible to generalize.

7. [Evaluating] What Are the Strengths of the Research Method?

The literature review provides an efficient way to assess researchers on their knowledge and understanding of a specific topic. Literature reviews can be conducted for almost any topic and may provide an in-depth overview of the topic. In addition, a literature review may offer a framework for research planning because researchers now have a clear idea of what has already been done in the academic field.

8. [Evaluating] What Are the Limitations of the Research Method?

The major limitation of this qualitative study is that only one elementary school was studied. The elementary school studied was located in a suburb, and among the teachers who were involved in this study, there were no teachers of color; therefore, diversity of the participants was limited.

9. [Evaluating] How Do You Judge the Validity of the Findings?

Although this study presents critical analysis of the literature, concerns still remain regarding the validity of the findings. The author did not clarify the selection criteria for the samples. For example, the author used the term "recent" instead of clarifying the range of the time period. Also, it is not clear how many articles were searched and selected based on the information provided by the author. The author should provide more information about the process of searching and selecting articles in order to generalize the findings. Also, it would be better for the author to provide more information about each study that was reviewed in this article (e.g. research methods, participants).

10. [Creating] How Can I Develop My Own Research Based on the Evaluation of the Reading?

This may be carried out by answering questions such as: What is a multi-dimensional lens? Can ethical issues be free from context? What about the following episode? Although it does not concern an ethical issue, it shows a strong perspective of relativism.

The psychologist Michael Cole and some colleagues once gave members of the Kpelle tribe, in Liberia, a version of the Wechsler Intelligence Scale for Children similarities test: they took a basket of food, tools, containers, and clothing and asked the tribesmen to sort them into appropriate categories. To the frustration of the researchers, the Kpelle chose functional pairings. They put a potato and a knife together because a knife is used to cut a potato. "A wise man could only do such-and-such," they explained. Finally, the researchers asked, "How would a fool do it?" The tribesmen immediate-

ly re-sorted the items into the *"right"* categories. *It can be argued that taxonomical categories are a developmental improvement—that is, that the Kpelle would be more likely to advance, technologically and scientifically, if they started to see the world that way. But to label them less intelligent than Westerners on the basis of their performance on that test is merely to state that they have different cognitive preferences and habits* (Gladwell, 2007).

Thus, I would like to investigate whether ethical issues can be judged in different ways based on the situation. On that basis, I would like to discuss the standards for determining educational leaders.

UNDERSTANDING FRAMEWORKS

Xiumin: "I have to choose one article and analyze the framework for the assignment. However, I don't have any clues about what the framework is."

Tao: "Yes, it is too vague. Also, all the professors told me that the framework is so important to both reading and writing. But I think the conclusions or the arguments of the paper are more important than the framework. During the classroom discussion, we always talked about the arguments of the paper. Why do we need to understand the framework?"

In the fable of "The Blind Men and the Elephant," several blind men touch different parts of an elephant and provide different perspectives about what the elephant is or looks like (see Figure 1.2). Although they present different understandings about what an elephant is like, they are all correct. Also, these men may find out the real nature of the elephant when they combine what they investigated. Researchers are like the blind men; they may not know or understand everything at once, but they have to explore the research question and collaborate with each other in order to understand the entirety of the research topic.

Figure 1.2. "The Blind Men and the Elephant."

To develop and understand what an elephant is and make the others touch the same part, however, each blind man needs to provide some clues about the part he is touching. For example, one blind man may explain, "I am down on my knees, and I touched some parts of the elephant on the ground. In this case, the elephant is a pillar." In order to have the same experiences as the blind man, you would have to get down on your knees and touch the parts of the elephant on the ground. Otherwise, you may not understand what parts of the elephant the blind man touched.

The role of the framework for the research is similar to the blind man's explanation about the characteristics of the elephant he touches. That is, a framework indicates the lens through which the researcher perceives the phenomenon; it provides organization of the problem under study regarding how various concepts, ideas, theories, or observable events are interrelated.

There are diverse types of frameworks (e.g. conceptual, theoretical, or philosophical), and sometimes the researcher uses multiple frameworks for one study because no single framework can handle all the issues related to the research question. For example, let us assume that you are the researcher who wants to evaluate elementary teachers' knowledge for teaching mathematics. In this case, there are several aspects of the study you have to frame before deciding on the research methods.

First, what is the concept of teaching? Does teaching indicate the actual instruction in a mathematics classroom, or does teaching include the process of preparing mathematics instruction? How about providing feedback on students' work after a mathematics class? Thus, you have to clearly state your concept of teaching in your conceptual framework. There is no single clearly defined concept of teaching. Based on the related studies, you may develop your own conceptual framework about the concept of teaching. In this case, there is a need for justification regarding why and how you develop your own conceptual framework. Or, you may apply other researchers' frameworks to your study. In both cases, your concept of teaching should be carried through to the end of the research.

Second, how do you evaluate teachers' knowledge for teaching mathematics? Are you going to develop test papers? Or are you going to observe the teachers' mathematics instruction? If you observe mathematics instruction, what will be the focus: the teacher's explanations or the students' participation? How about student outcomes as evidence of a teacher's knowledge for teaching mathematics? In this case, various approaches would be acceptable if an appropriate basis for your methodology was provided. Although the research question plays a vital role in deciding the research design and methodology (National Research Council, 2002), the framework also provides a basis for the research method. For example, consider Vygotsky's theory that learning is compatible with adult guidance, especially guidance as to how teachers use language in the classroom (e.g., Vygotsky, 1978; 1997).

According to Vygotsky, teachers' use of language plays a pivotal role in students' intellectual development and success in learning content, because teachers' use of language guides students' mathematics understanding and thinking (Albert, 2012; Chaiklin, 1986). Thus, Vygotsky's perspective that language is an essential tool for learning and understanding content may serve as a model for developing the theoretical framework for your study about teachers' use of language during mathematics instruction. In this case, you may develop your research methods based on your theoretical framework. Also, the findings from your study should be understood within the theoretical framework.

In the same way, if appropriate, you may develop a philosophical or another applicable framework for the research you are investigating. Developing an understanding of frameworks for various empirical studies reviewed by authors or researchers will help you see potential relationships across the various studies. Understanding the framework, be it conceptual or theoretical, can help you make sense of authors' research questions, rationale, and methodology. This can also help you when you are ready to develop your own framework and research questions.

Also, when you read an article, you may evaluate the validity of the research methods or findings based on the framework as defined by the researcher. For example, if the researcher defined the concepts of teaching as the range of three instructional stages—preparing, actual teaching, and providing feedback on students' work—then the research methods should address how to obtain data related to these instructional steps. Also, the discussion of findings should be about the relationship between teachers' knowledge for teaching mathematics at each instructional stage. Although the research questions may be similar, if the frameworks are dissimilar, then it will be important to remember that the findings for one study may differ from those of another study. Also, as you read and review research articles and book chapters, you may develop ideas for your own research.

FINDING RELATIONSHIPS ACROSS ARGUMENTS IN VARIOUS ARTICLES

Tanabat: "I don't know why the professor gave us these articles."

Onsa: "What do you mean? You mean the articles were poorly developed?"

Tanabat: "No, each article is great. However, they are about different topics. Also, I don't know how they fit the theme of the course. The professor always gives us more than five articles to read for each class meeting. It took a lot of time to finish the readings. What is worse, I don't understand why I should read these articles."

At the graduate level, each course requires students to read several articles or a book for each class, which means absorbing between 50 to 200 pages of work. This amount of reading per week is definitely challenging for international students. In some cases, the number of pages that one is required to read might double or triple, if a similar amount is assigned for two or more classes. What is worse, sometimes students do not know why they have to read so many articles every week.

International students soon learn that that there are more required readings at the graduate level than at the undergraduate level. For undergraduate students, professors give students articles to provide a context from which theories and concepts emerge. On the other hand, for graduate students, professors offer the list of readings so that students may develop their own critical perspectives. The following episode refers to an example reading at the graduate level.

Student: "I need your help. I don't know how these articles fit today's topic. I read four articles out of the five that you gave to me."

Professor: "Which article didn't you read?"

Student: "The first one from the list. I read from two to five."

Professor: "Why did you skip the first one on the list?"

Student: "Because it looked longer than the others. I started with the short one."

Professor: "Why did you change the order of the readings? There is a reason why I put the articles in order. The first one is the most important article for today's class. The other four articles are examples that apply the concepts from the first article in diverse ways. That's why you can't find any connections among the articles. I can't help you at this moment because you didn't read the most important article, and therefore, you don't understand the concepts."

The academic field is a community of new thought. As a doctoral student and an emerging scholar, you should know how to discuss the major concepts and research of academic fields. One way to do so is to find connections among articles. Sometimes authors present opposing arguments, or corresponding ideas, by providing academic evidence for each of them. By focusing on the relationship among articles, you can practice finding meaningful implications from the studies for your own research.

Thus, some professors want graduate students to practice finding connections among articles from the required readings. There are diverse ways of arranging articles or books to assist you in making connections. The following examples show the ways that professors arrange articles for a class.

To Provide Example of Major Concepts

The most common way of arranging articles is to place them around the major article, which provides the target topic for the class. In this case, the major article is placed first on the list of required readings. The major article provides explanations about the main concepts for the course (see Figure 1.3). The sub-articles may be research articles that apply the major concepts of the main article. In this case, professors require in-depth understanding of the main concepts.

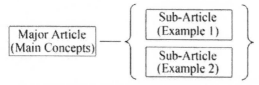

Figure 1.3. The Relationships among Articles (1).

Occasionally, professors provide examples with counterexamples in order to show how main concepts influence other research (see Figure 1.4). In this case, you need to focus on the differences between the examples and the counterexamples. Also, it is helpful to analyze the strengths and weaknesses of the examples and counterexamples, as well as understanding the main concepts.

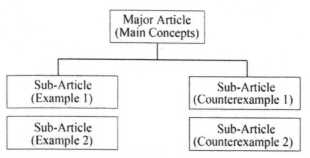

Figure 1.4. The Relationships among Articles (2).

To Ask about Your Positionality as a Researcher

Occasionally, professors provide lists of readings without a major article. When the lesson covers controversial topics or discussions about specific phenomena, professors offer related articles in order to provide students with different types of intellectual nourishment (see Figure 1.5). It may be hard for students to find the relationship without reading the main article. In this case, you need to confirm and focus on the topic in the syllabus as you read the article.

In this case, you need to analyze the strengths and weaknesses of each opinion as you read the articles. Also, as a student, you are expected to decide where you stand as a researcher. You should think about what kinds of evidence are needed to support your opinion or positionality, and to critique the opinions of others. The relevant point is that positionality is a key characteristic of our identity, in which "our gender, our race, our class, our age . . . are markers of relational positions rather than essential qualities. Their effects and implications change according to context" (Tetreault, 1993, p. 139).

Sometimes you will be required to understand the complexity of the phenomena within the readings (see Figure 1.6). When you read articles, you may ask: "What perspective is missing from these diverse viewpoints? Which viewpoint is closer to my own stance as a researcher?"

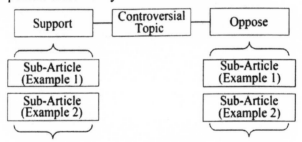

Figure 1.5.   The Relationships among Articles (3).

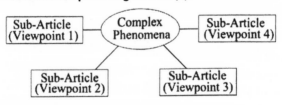

Figure 1.6.   The Relationships among Articles (4).

To Provide Historical Context for the Concepts

Occasionally, the articles are listed in chronological order (see Figure 1.7). In this case, you are required to understand their historical context. More to the point, you have to connect how these historical contexts affect current phenomena. Also, you may think about what is needed in order to change current phenomena, based on your understanding of the historical context.

Figure 1.7. The Relationships among Articles (5).

As noted above, it is not easy to find the relationship among articles. Although this book presents several examples of arranging articles, professors provide lists of readings in diverse ways based on their instructional purpose. For example, there was a professor who required students to read one of his articles for the first lesson of the course, although the article seemed like it was not related to the course. He explained that he wanted to introduce himself by showcasing a major research focus of his work.

Thus, it is suggested that you check the topic of the lesson and the order of the reading from the syllabus. Although in most cases the relationships among articles may not be explicitly stated in the syllabus, you may arrange articles in diverse ways and find the relationships by focusing on the topic of the lesson. Also, it is suggested that you create a study group and discuss these relationships before the lesson. If you cannot find the relationships after doing all of this, you can ask professors about their intentions regarding the readings.

DEVELOPING AND WRITING SUMMARIES

Choi: "I was surprised that you did well during the classroom discussion. Your English was not perfect, but I liked the fact that you gave us an example from the readings when you explained your idea. How were you able to remember what you read from so many articles?"

Luhan: "Well, I usually read articles twice before class, and I make notes about the article as I read it."

Choi: "Twice? That's scary! I usually skim through the articles and check only the topic before class."

We have heard some students complain that "U.S. professors give us so many articles to read, but do not provide clear explanations during class. Sometimes I feel it is a waste of time to sit in a classroom and listen to the other students' meaningless words. I want to learn from the professor! Not from the students!"

Students should understand why the professor assigns them so many articles to read. As noted in a previous section, professors expect students to read articles critically. Professors assume that graduate students enter programs with the knowledge base of how to read for understanding, select the main ideas, and remember these major ideas as they are presented in research articles and other academic readings. In other words, a professor enters the classroom assuming that students already understand the major concepts of the topic of discussion. During the discussion, a professor expects students to engage in discourse about what they found relevant from applying, analyzing, and evaluating the reading, as well from as creating their own ideas. Thus, students should have a grasp of the main concepts before the class meets, and understand the major topics that are discussed there. Of course, if they cannot understand the topics, they may ask their professor during the discussion. Fully understanding and then remembering every concept presented or discussed in a course will take time.

A useful technique that you may have learned in high school or during your undergraduate studies is writing an article summary, often referred to as an abstract. Writing a summary for each article is a good approach to understanding and remembering the main concepts of the articles. It is also helpful in finding the relationship among articles. You probably have had an experience in which you were not able to remember the content of the first article, when you were in the process of reading the second one. When you make a summary, you don't need to read the first article again. You can use the summary when you participate in the class discussion. The way to draw on what you have read before class and apply it during the discussion will be considered in the following chapter.

When you make a summary, you may add notes regarding your own ideas, questions, or critiques. Your notes will be helpful during class discussions as well as when you write a paper for the course; your notes may provide some clues for developing your thinking for the paper.

We suggest that you check the authors' names when you make a summary. In addition, you need to check the authors cited in the article. In the United States, professors and students use the author's name instead of the book or article title when they mention a written source.

Sometimes the summary will not be enough for your discussion or writing; thus, you will need to check the original content. If you include a page number with your summary, it might be helpful for you in finding what you need. Checking the year when the article was published is also recommended (see Box 1.1).

For all its usefulness, it is not easy to prepare a summary for each reading. This is especially the case when the usual course load for graduate students is three courses each semester. Therefore, it may be impossible for international students to write summaries of each article for every course. Many students, including U.S. graduate students, find this process too challenging, so we strongly recommend that you form study-groups with your classmates. In your study-group, you may share summaries with your group members. As you engage in discussions during meeting time, it might be helpful for you to work with your group members to find relevant relationships among the assigned articles. Additionally, you can practice your academic speech during discussion with your study-group. Therefore, it will be valuable to have a study-group that includes U.S. students as well as international students.

Box 1.1. Example of a Summary

Summary pages 3-29
- Fenstermacher, a philosopher of education, has set out to review the ideas about knowledge from within the field of research on teaching.
- He is interested in how notions of knowledge are used and analyzed in a number of research programs that study teachers and their teaching.
- He examines how the knowledge teachers generate through experience differs from that generated by those who study research on teaching.
- There are two bodies of this research on teacher knowledge: CONVENTIONAL SCIENTIFIC APPROACHES & ALTERNATIVE APPROACHES.
- This chapter focuses on the "epistemological aspects" of research programs that claim to be about teacher knowledge. According to the author, epistemological aspects are, "...those features of the research that assert or imply notions about the nature of knowledge" (Fenstermacher, 1994, p. 4).
- In examining this literature, the author asks, "who is the knower and what does the knower know?" (Fenstermacher, 1994, p. 5).

[An overview of the teacher knowledge literature]
There are four questions that guided the literature review..

1. What is known about effective teaching? (Conventional behavioral science research, process-product, TK/F – teacher knowledge: formal)
2. What do teachers know (related to a teacher's experiences, TK/P – teacher knowledge: practical)?
3. What knowledge is essential for teaching?
4. Who produces knowledge about teaching (disparity between researchers' knowledge and teachers' knowledge)?

Also, not every class at the graduate level requires summaries for readings. Usually, when you take a seminar course, you need to prepare summaries for class discussions. You will need to investigate and find out what the courses require.

BIBLIOGRAPHY

Albert, L. R. *Rhetorical Ways of Thinking: Vygotskian Theory and Mathematical Learning.* New York: Springer, 2012.

Bloom, B. *Taxonomy of Educational Objectives, Handbook I: The Cognitive Domain.* New York: David McKay, 1956.

Chaiklin, S. "Constructing Productions and Producing Constructions." *The American Psychologist,* 41 no. 5 (1986): 590-593.

Fenstermacher, G. "The Knower and the Known: The Nature of Knowledge in Research on Teaching." In *Review of Research in Education,* Edited by L. Darling-Hammond. Vol. 20, pp. 3–56. Washington, DC: American Educational Research Association, 1994.

Gladwell, M. "None of the Above; What I.Q. Doesn't Tell You About Race." *The New Yorker,* 2007. http://www.newyorker.com/arts/critics/books/2007/12/17/071217crbo_books_glad well?printable=true. Accessed September 9, 2013.

National Research Council. *Scientific Research in Education.* Washington, DC: National Academy Press, 2002.

Tetreault, M. K. T. "Classrooms for Diversity: Rethinking Curriculum and Pedagogy." In *Multicultural Education: Issues and Perspectives,* 2nd ed. Edited by J. A Banks & C. A. M. Banks, pp. 129–148. Boston: Allyn & Bacon, 1993.

Vygotsky. L.S. *Mind in Society: The Development of Higher Psychological Processes.* Cambridge: Harvard University Press, 1978.

———. "Genesis of Higher Mental Functions." In *The Collected Works of L. S. Vygotsky.* Edited by R. W. Rieber. Vol. 4. New York: Plenum, 1997. (Original work published 1931.)

Chapter Two

Engaging in Academic Discussions

INTRODUCTION

Classroom discussion is not a mere question-and-answer session. In fact, discourse in a classroom is a collaborative thought process. Participating in collaborative thought requires certain skills. In this chapter, we offer practical tips for participating in classroom discussions; these include how to use starter sentences and how to develop grounds for arguments from your readings.

PROVIDE GROUNDS FOR YOUR STATEMENTS

Landicho: "Whenever I say something, the professor asks me to verify my statements. I have no idea what he is saying. The idea just originates up in my head. How can I verify my thinking process?"

Moses: "I try to say something at least once in class in order to get points for discussion. However, the professor gives me feedback, stating that my participation is weak. I cannot speak as fluently as the U.S. students. It is frustrating. I will not be able to get an A in the course, which penalizes lack of participation due to my poor English speaking ability."

Sometimes, international students who are not familiar with classroom discussion are embarrassed by open-ended discussions in U.S. courses. Some students seem to think that they can say anything to engage in the discussion, and therefore, do not take time to organize their thoughts. Other students decide to sit quietly in class because they believe that they cannot follow the discussion due to their lack of English proficiency. If a percentage of your final grade for the course requires active participation in course discussions, then both of these cases may result in lowering of your final grade because of inappropriate comments or lack of engagement during course discussions.

For students who misunderstand the importance of participating in discussions, it is recommended that they consider the purpose of the discussion at the beginning of the course. The aims of academic discussions are to broaden our understanding of the lesson topic, and to find meaningful implications from what we read and learn in class. Thus, students' comments during a discussion should correspond with its purpose.

In order to make meaningful and helpful comments to other classmates, students should provide grounds for their comments, thoughts, or ideas. For example, let's think about the phrase "I like your idea." In day-to-day conversation, it could be used as a way of complimenting others' ideas, and you may not need to explain why an idea appeals to you. But in academic discussions, you need to state a reason why you like the idea. This is because the most important point of your comment, in an academic context, is not the fact that you like an idea but the reason why you like it. When you state this reason, the other students may derive some implications from your comment.

There are two ways to provide grounds for your comments, thoughts, or ideas. First, you may cite your own experiences. For example, you may say, "I like your idea that students need to understand the mathematics concepts. I observed a student who solved an addition problem without regrouping correctly. However, he can't solve the addition problem without regrouping correctly. He did not understand the basic concept of regrouping, although he knew the procedural rules of addition." Second, you may provide grounds based on what you took from the required reading. For instance, you may say, "I like your idea that students need to understand the mathematics concepts. Skemp's research points out that students who have a conceptual understanding tend to learn faster than those who do not, when they learn new mathematics concepts." A detailed explanation for both cases will be presented in the following sections.

Students with low English proficiency may use certain strategies in order to express themselves clearly during the discussion. One of the strategies is to use *starter sentences*, which will be discussed in the following section. Starter sentences help your audience get the point of your comments by providing a clue about what you are going to say. Another strategy is to ask questions. This is a good way to participate in the discussion, especially for international students who are not familiar with the topic or whose English proficiency is low. In addition, a good question could help the other students' understanding of the topic.

At the beginning of the lecture, professors usually ask, "Are there any questions about your readings?" Also, they will ask questions during or at the end of the class in order to check students' understanding. You may notice that this is a good time to ask your questions. You should prepare your questions based on the reading, before class. Also, you may note some questions while you are listening to the lecture or to the other students' discussion points. International students who fear participating in discussions may improve their confidence by asking a single question during class.

In both of these cases, international students should know that they should be careful about using idioms from their own country. Sometimes, international students use translated idioms during discussions. An idiom is a combination of words that has a figurative meaning based on its common usage. Thus, people who are not familiar with the idiom may not understand its true meaning. Similarly, students should be careful when using figures of speech, such as similes, metaphors, or idiomatic expressions.

USE YOUR OWN EXPERIENCES FOR YOUR ARGUMENTS

Ahmet: "I don't know why the school admits international students. When I take the class, nobody asks me about my country or my own perspectives. They always talk about the United States."

Murat: "Sometimes, I feel like classroom discussions are a waste of time. The U.S. students always talk about their personal experiences during discussions. I don't understand why I have to hear their personal stories. I want to learn something from the professor who has a rich knowledge base and experiences in the academic field. What is worse, when I try to tell my own story, nobody seems to care about it. I think . . . they believe that their experiences are worth more than the experiences of international students."

Let's think about Cho's experiences in the United States in order to understand the importance of background when you engage in conversation with others. Cho came to the United States about a year ago to start a doctoral degree at a university. Her cohorts invited her to dinner. The dinner was nice, but she could not follow the conversation from time to time. For example, one of her friends mentioned, "The Big Bang Theory," which is a famous TV comedy show in the United States. Everyone at the table seemed to be aware of the comedy show and was able to contribute to the conversation regarding a recent episode. Cho was not able to contribute because she had never watched the show before. Cho wanted to talk about a famous drama from her own country, but she gave up trying because she thought that they were not aware of Korean dramas.

When you have conversations with your friends, consider whether your friends are familiar with the topic. If your friends do not know about the topic, you may need to provide extra explanations or background information about the topic in order to engage them in conversation about the topic as well as to help them understand it.

Academic discussions in a classroom may be understood in the same way. When the U.S. students talk about their personal experiences, the professor or the other students may understand what the students are saying. Without extra explanation, they know how it relates to the topic of discussion because they share a similar cultural background and experiences. The following episode shows the importance of a shared culture.

Professor: "So far, we have been exploring educational policy. The teachers' pay is to be tied to their performance, which is decided by their students' academic achievement score."

U.S. Student: "One of my friends who works as a mathematics teacher in a public high school is always worried about MCAS [the Massachusetts Comprehensive Assessment System]. So, she teaches from a math workbook developed from TIMSS [Trends in International Mathematics and Science Study] test items during her class."

South Korean Student: "The teacher-union should do something in order to prevent the policy. We had a similar issue in South Korea. The government provided bonuses to teachers based on their performance at their school. So, the teachers sent their bonuses to one of the major teacher-unions. The teacher-union sent it to the government. Finally, the government had to change the policy. The U.S. teachers should do something like that."

MCAS is a high-stakes test given by school districts in the Northeastern U.S. state of Massachusetts. American students who are not education majors (or who do not have much interest in Massachusetts) may not know about MCAS. Thus, this example illustrates that students' backgrounds are not just an issue for international students. Assuming, however, that the U.S. students were familiar with MCAS, we notice that the U.S. student tried to explain the adverse effects of the educational policy by introducing her friend's story. The U.S. student suggested, "a teacher in a public high school is not teaching mathematics concepts in a class but rather focusing on how to improve her students' scores on high-stakes tests. It is a problem that is caused by the policy." The U.S. professor and students understood the meaning of the story, because they were cognizant of MCAS and teaching workbooks in a mathematics class, based on their school experiences in the United States. In this case, if the South Korean student did not know about MCAS, the story told by the U.S. student might be meaningless.

On the other hand, it may be difficult for the U.S. professor and students to understand the South Korean student's story, although stated clearly by the student. Unlike in the United States, in South Korea the government hires public school teachers. Also, there are robust teacher-unions, which have political power. If U.S. students are not familiar with the educational context of South Korea, they will not understand the implications of the South Korean student's story. In this case, if the topic of the class covers the role of teacher unions, the professor or U.S. students should ask the student about the teacher-union system in South Korea. But there is the likelihood that the South Korean student will not receive any feedback from the class.

If the professor or the students in your class are interested in cases from your own country, or your own perspectives as an international student, you do not need to worry about the other students' backgrounds. They are willing to listen to your story and will ask questions if they do not understand what you are saying. When you present cases from your own country during the general classroom discussion, however, you should consider the following questions.

Is My Story Related to the Topic Being Discussed?

You should consider how your story is connected to the broader topic of the discussion. As seen in the previous episode, if the topic covers the role of teacher-unions in educational policy, the South Korean student's statement would contribute to the discussion. However, if not, the student should focus on the right function or adverse effect of the policy.

Is the Class Wondering about Diverse Cases from Different Countries?

When the class is willing to know about your country, you definitely should introduce your own experiences. In this case, the class will ask and provide feedback regarding your statements. You should remember, however, that you are only one student in a classroom, even though you might be the only international student. In some cases, the class may not be interested in your story.

Did I Provide Enough Information for the Class to Understand My Story?

Because students in your course may not know much about your country, it will be important to provide contextual information that might assist them in understanding your story. Thus, when you introduce your case or tell a story, you should consider the essential information your audience needs to know. Also, it will be essential that you do not dominate the discussion. Some international students spend too much time on their story in order to provide the background of the story. The key is to find the right balance regarding how much context and information is needed, so that it does not appear like you are giving a lecture. You want to keep the students engaged and interested in your comments.

You should understand that there is a possibility the professor and the U.S. students may not give any feedback or comments on your statement because they may not know how to respond. Sometimes, U.S. students may not understand international students' comments, questions, or stories offered during the discussion. Furthermore, some international students may not understand why the U.S. students talk about their personal experiences during class. Of course, the U.S. professor and students should try to understand the international students' perspectives. Yet international students should also practice delivering their own stories efficiently during discussions.

DEVELOP YOUR IDEAS FROM THE READINGS

Mao: "There is a brilliant international student in my class. Her English is not perfect, but she always provides the right comments regarding the classroom discussion. Whenever she says something, every student in the class listen to her. She leads the entire discussion, although she is an international student. She is amazing."

Yukiko: "I received feedback from the professor that I need to improve my discussion technique by providing meaningful statements. My oral English is not good. How can I contribute to the class and engage in discussions like the U.S. students?"

As noted in the previous section, international students may have difficulty sharing their experiences in U.S. classrooms. So, how can international students participate effectively in class discussions?

The key to effective participation is in the list of required readings the professor provides. Depending on the professor's instructional aims, these readings serve several purposes. One of the common reasons to provide readings might be to help students understand concepts deeply. Another reason might be to provide contextual and intellectual scaffolding for students in order to help them prepare for class discussion.

Based on the readings, a discussion provides both international and U.S. students with an equal chance to participate in class discussions. The readings provide all students in the class with the same critical information about a topic. In this case, discussions based on the readings go beyond a simple explanation of the concepts or cases. In other words, you have to understand the concept and use it to ground your statements.

Let's look at Hwang's case. Hwang reads a book related to school leadership. From the book, he learns that school leaders should consider diverse aspects of school management. For example, school leaders should create an educational environment in the school and interact with teachers. Also, the school leaders should know school structures and how to manage the system. During the classroom discussion, the professor asks the students, "What if the school board selects Bill Gates as a school leader. What do you think about that? Do you agree or disagree with the school board's decision?' The students start to discuss the situation as follows.

Jim: "I do not agree with the school board's decision, because Bill Gates is not an educator."

Professor: "Should only educators be school leaders? Do you have any evidence that might prove that educators are better school leaders than who those are not educators?"

Jim: "No . . . but he does not know education."

Professor: "Who said that? Who said that he does not know education? Actually, he has a great interest in the educational field."

Jim: ". . . "

Hwang: "This book states that school leaders should know how to manage school systems and how to create educational environments. Creating educational environments cannot be explained by just economic principles. For example, the school leader should understand the moral issues in the educational field. I think Bill Gates would succeed in managing a school system because he proves his ability from his own business. However, we are not sure that he knows that there are diverse things to consider, including ethical problems for educational issues."

Professor: "Are you saying that you are agreeing with the decision?"

Hwang: "In terms of school management, yes. But, for educational aspects, we need more investigation."

Kate: "I agree with Hwang's point that there are two aspects of school management. When I read the book..."

How do you evaluate this discussion? Basically, both Jim and Hwang pointed out that the school board should consider that Bill Gates is not an educator. Yet they each presented their opinions in a different way. While Jim gave his personal perspective without verification, Hwang related his idea to what was explained in the book. Hwang did not need to provide an explanation about "ethical problems for educational issues" because the book already described it. Without a specific explanation of ethical problems, Hwang was able to verify his idea because everyone in the class had already read the same book. Therefore, Kate was able to respond to Hwang's idea and confirm it by mentioning the same book.

What if Hwang's argument had been based on his own his experiences from his country, as follows?

Hwang: "In my country, the school can invite an expert as their school leader. An expert does not have to be an educator. I heard that the school invited an expert who was not an educator. However, the school started to have so many problems because the leader was not an educator. For example, his major concern was about students' academic achievement, rather than the virtue of the educational process. I think a similar issue may arise if Bill Gates becomes a school leader."

Based on Hwang's comments, the class might wonder if his experience from his country can be generalized to the United States. Some students may wonder about the process of inviting experts. But they probably would not ask about it, because the questions do not fit the topic of the discussion. Some students might think that it is all right to be concerned about students' achievement. Still, they would probably hesitate to provide feedback, because they do not have any information about the educational context of Hwang's country. In this case, Hwang's comment is acceptable in class discussion, but might fail to provide a meaningful implication for the other students.

Another merit of referencing readings during class discussion is to camouflage your level of English speaking. As noted earlier, you need to provide context in order to use cases from your country for class discussion. Yet for international students whose English is not flawless, it may not be easy to provide coherent explanations about their country. On the other hand, if you speak based on the readings, you won't need to explain what you read, because everyone in the class has read it as well. Thus, you can state your argument clearly and briefly by drawing from your readings.

During the lesson, you should make a connection between your argument and the reading, based on the question posed by the professor. In order to use what you read when you engage in class discussion, you should have a strong understanding of the reading. You may notice that even U.S. students make summaries of readings, or read the articles several times in order to remember and to understand the content of the readings. You have to realize that no satisfactory discussion can be carried out without work.

USE STARTER SENTENCES

Yuri: "I really want to participate in class discussion. However, before I can complete what I am trying to say, I am interrupted by another student. Or whenever I do have the chance to complete my comments, the class's response is silence. Also, the professor does not provide any comments. I think he does not understand my comment. His usual response is 'Ok. That's good. Does anyone else have something to say?' Such a response makes me think he is ignoring me and disrespects me."

Ivan: "In my case, I can't keep up with the discussion. When I try to offer a comment in response to another student's statement, several students quickly offer their opinions before I start to talk. When it is my turn to talk, I can't say what I wanted to say because someone else has already mentioned something similar to my idea, and I don't want it to appear as though I do not have my own opinion."

For many international students, it may be difficult to participate in a class discussion. It is a challenge for international students to think about a topic while they are trying to understand other students' comments in English at the same time. What is worse is that it may be difficult for international students to get into the discussion naturally. For example, some international students must first listen to what is being said in English. Second, they make a mental translation to their first language, and then translate their response or comment into English. The discussion can move very quickly, and if you struggle with speaking English, then your participation may not be as active as you would like.

Furthermore, there are other international students who are not able to participate in class discussion because they do not know how to get involved. In cases like these, they are only able to participate in the discussion when they are asked a specific question by the professor. Also, it is a challenge for some U.S. professors and students to understand what international students say during discussions. You may notice that U.S. students engage in discussions with a sense of ease and effectiveness. How is this possible? When you observe them, you may find that they may begin their comments with *starter sentences*, which make connections between various comments, statements, or opinions provided by students. Also, the starter sentences provide some clues about the comment they are about to make. If you use starter sentences, it may help listeners anticipate what you are about to say, and help them prepare appropriate responses to your comments. Some examples of starter sentences and their practical uses are as follows.

I Am Sorry. I Think I Missed Something. May I Ask a Question?

When you listen to a lecture, you may have a question. But most international students who use English as their second language hesitate to ask the professor a question because they are not sure whether the professor has already explained it or not; they are not sure whether they have a question because the professor did not explain it or because they did not understand the English explanation. In the United States, it is O.K. to ask a question about the professor's explanation or statement. Yet international students may be afraid of giving the impression that they do not understand English. Also, these students may not know how to ask a question appropriately. They do not want to say, "I don't understand what you are saying."

In this case, you can use the sentence, *"I am sorry. I think I missed something. May I ask a question?"* Then, the professor will probably say, "Sure, go ahead." The expectation is that you will ask a question relevant to the lecture. If you missed something addressed in the lecture, the professor will provide the information again. If your question is about a point that was not made, then the professor will provide additional information to answer your question.

I Have a Question, but I Am Not Sure It Relates to the Topic. May I Ask?

Use this sentence for a question that digresses from the main topic of the discussion. For example, during the discussion about strengths and weaknesses of the teacher evaluation system, you wondered about how U.S teachers perceive the evaluation system. You were not sure whether you could ask a related question because it was not about those strengths and weaknesses. In this case, use the starter sentence given above, which may indicate that you are going to say something different from the main topic of the discussion.

Also, you may use starter sentences when you present a differing opinion in a gentle way. It is important that you try not to engage in arguments that are counterproductive. Some international students start to argue, stating, "I don't think so" or "I don't agree with you." This approach is not wrong; however, it might appear to be somewhat aggressive and impolite. Starting with a question provides an opportunity for you to get into the discussion more gently. For example, one of the lectures Kim attended focused on the special education idea of *slow learning*. The professor explained the concepts of *slow learning,* comparing it to fast food and slow food. The major point of his argument was to focus on the quality of education rather than on achievement tests. While Kim was listening, she was wondering whether or not *fast learning* is always bad. She wanted to ask the professor this, but did not want to argue with him. Thus, she started the conversation with the starter sentence as follows.

> Kim: *"I have a question, but I am not sure it relates to the topic. May I ask?"*

> Professor: *"Sure, go ahead."*

> Kim: *"Is fast learning always worse than slow learning?"*

> Professor: *"What do you mean? Slow does not mean lazy or late in this case."* (He probably assumed that Kim misunderstood him because Kim is an international student.)

> Kim: *"I know. But. . . ."*

> Professor: *"O.K. Can you explain why you think so?"*

> Kim: *"Yes, since the Korean War, about 50 years ago, South Korea's education system has applied fast learning to develop as a country, becoming one of the leading industrialized countries in the world. Developing countries and third world countries may need fast learning more than they might need the slow learning system. What do you think?"*

When you discuss classroom topics in a small group, you may use a different starter sentence. In this case, you can simply say, "May I ask a question?" After stating the starter sentence, you may point out what the other students missed during the discussion. For example, you might ask, "What about the strengths of fast learning? I think that fast learning has its own strengths, too." In this case, you may use another starter sentence, *"I agree with Kim about. . . . However, I have a question about one of the points she made. . . ."*

Back to Jane's Point. . . .

One of the most embarrassing situations for international students is when the topic changes during the discussion, and the student is not aware of it. For example, during a class discussion about how to develop good research questions, Jane provided an example of a research question. Yan, along with several other students, raised her hand, and the professor called on several of these students but not Yan. These students offered suggestions about how to improve the question posed by Jane, and they also commented on the importance of selecting appropriate research methods, which resulted in a shift in the discussion; the focus was then on research methods and not research questions.

Finally, Yan was recognized by the professor and made a comment that related directly to the development of good research questions. She was embarrassed when she realized that although her comment was relevant to the previous topic, the class discussion had shifted. The students and the professor were no longer discussing research questions; therefore, her comment did not fit the flow of the discussion because the topic had changed. Also, the professor and the other students did not know how to respond to Yan's comment.

If you use the starter sentence, you can turn the topic back to the original one. You may start your comments with a summary of Jane's argument. For example, you might say, "*In regards to Jane's example of a good research question, I think. . . .* " Or, you can use another starter sentence: "*I am sorry but I was thinking about Jane's earlier example. May I add some points to her argument?*" If you use the starter sentence, you can say what you wanted to say without cutting off the discussion. In this case, the purpose of the starter sentence is to introduce what you are going to say and help your audience understand your comment.

May I Add an Example about Indonesia?

An important strength of international students is their international viewpoints and examples. International students may contribute to discussions by using their international experience. When the professor explains the concepts of a topic, you may find examples or counterexamples from your own experience. When you find a relevant example and want to add it to the discussion, you may start your comments with, "*May I add an example about Indonesia?*"

This section presented some examples of starter sentences. You may find other starter sentences for various situations when you observe class discussions. You may make notes about what you find and use them later. You will need to put a lot of effort towards learning the rules of a discussion. Be sure to put the starter sentences in your own words, so you can use them naturally.

Also, you may find that some U.S. students start their discussion without starter sentences. The role of the starter sentences is to help you initiate your statement, when you are unsure how to start. Thus, you do not need to use starter sentences all the time. However, appropriate use of starter sentences will help you engage in class discussions naturally.

IMPROVE YOUR CLASSROOM PARTICIPATION

Sinan: "I just stay quiet during class discussion. I did not participate in class discussions when I was in my own country. Also, there were not many class discussions where I came from. I don't know why U.S. professors force me to speak during class. I think professors should respect cultural differences."

Altan: "I don't like to talk in front of many students. Speaking English in front of native speakers is fearful to me. I am afraid that everyone in class, including the professor, is going to ignore me after they listen to my poor English. In fact, I usually give up my participation points for class discussion. It would be better for me to focus on writing papers."

International students who do not want to participate in academic discussions have their own reasons for not participating. Some of the students may not participate due to fear and anxiety about being viewed as unintelligent because of their English speaking skills. Others may not have had much experience engaging in class discussions because it may not have been a common practice in their country. Thus, if part of their final grade for a course includes points for participation, they are willing to give them up and accept a lower final grade.

It might seem natural for some international students to struggle with how to participate in classroom discussions. Although some international students may score high on the Speaking Section of the Test of English as a Foreign Language (TOEFL), they are likely to experience difficulty in the classroom, because there are distinct differences between informal conversation and academic discussions. For academic discussions, international students should know how to present their ideas logically, applying appropriate academic language that is specific to the discipline they are studying. Also, they need to be aware that there are certain norms in academic discussions, which will be discussed below.

For all the difficulties academic discussions might present, the aspiration is that international students will not give up the opportunity to engage in these discussions. Graduate school is an excellent opportunity for you to learn about and engage in academic discussions. Although there might be various reasons why international students come to study in the United States, one of the major reasons is to become a scholar with a global perspective. Furthermore, if international students are studying to become scholars and leaders in their chosen field, they should know that such an endeavor requires involvement in international conferences, seminars, and symposiums, where English is the primary language.

To engage effectively in academic discussions, students need to learn how to participate. A meaningful way to do this is to practice interacting with other students. For example, when Jackie entered her doctoral studies, she had a difficult time participating in academic discussions. It was a great challenge for her to follow and engage in the course discussions. This aspect provided a learning curve for her; she realized that it was going to take time for her to take an active part in academic discussions. After a conversation with her advisor, Jackie developed a plan that would assist her in learning how to participate in classroom discussions (see Figure 2.1).

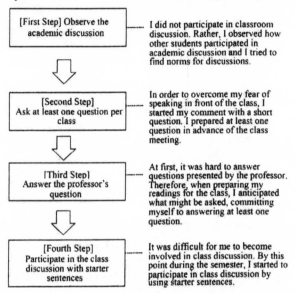

Figure 2.1.   A Plan for Participating in Classroom Discussion.

Figure 2.1 shows Jackie's progression throughout the semester, indicating how she strategically planned and engaged in academic discussions. In this fashion, she participated in her own way. For the first semester, she was slow in putting her plan into action, which led to her losing participation points and the resulting grades being lower than expected. For the next academic term, she used the plan in a more efficient way, by observing less and spending more time asking and answering questions. It is important to note that one comment or question during the class discussion will not guarantee you an A. Keep in mind, however, that you are in graduate school because you want to learn. Also, you should know that grades are not the only significant thing about you. Thus, you should develop your own plan based on your personality and English level. If you do not try, you will gain nothing.

Chapter Three

Writing at the Academic Level

INTRODUCTION

As a graduate student, you will be required to write a variety of academic papers. Some of these papers require framing your composition around an argument or problem. Others may require writing from the perspective of a critical question. This section will consider what an academic paper might involve if developed around a specific research question. In order to write a paper, students should understand that there are internal and external rules for writing. Internal rules will help you organize your ideas and the grounds for your arguments coherently, based on a research question that you want to investigate in your paper. External rules refer to the requirement that your writing must follow an academic format, such as American Psychological Association (APA) style. Figure 3.1 shows the general rules for an academic paper.

In this chapter, we discuss how to write a paper according to academic standards, which may be applied to various U.S. fields of study. Please note, however, that this chapter does not cover general rules for good writing, such as grammar and sentence structure. Rather, this chapter focuses on writing papers at the graduate level, in which the primary aim is to develop a paper based on a research question.

THE SIGNIFICANCE OF THE RESEARCH QUESTION

Yen: "I thought I wrote the paper pretty well. I analyzed the historical background of a current social phenomenon in my country. I also added how we may overcome the current social issue. However, the professor's feedback stated that my paper was not well organized."

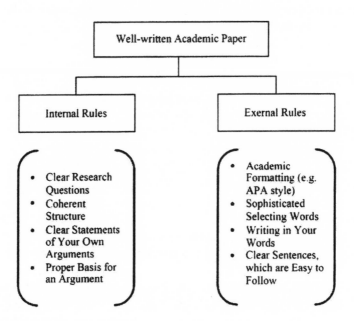

Figure 3.1.   An Academic Paper.

Cheng: "I also received a B in the course. I spent one month writing the paper. But the professor said that my research question was vague. I did not conduct research for my paper. It was just an analysis of a movie. Why do I need a research question?"

In some countries, the word *research* only refers to conducting empirical studies that need qualitative or quantitative data. If international students share this perspective, they are likely to confuse the *topic* and the *research question* when writing a paper for their coursework. These students believe that they have to write a paper about the topic, thinking that a research question applies only to their dissertation or a large research project. This misunderstanding can lead to writing an academic paper that seems vague and unorganized.

Writing at the graduate level requires a systemic and in-depth approach toward a topic. In order to understand writing at the graduate level, you have to recognize the difference between *topic* and *research*. The term *topic* represents the subject or theme under consideration, while the term *research* indicates a systematic investigation of a certain topic. Thus, to conduct research does not always require empirical data. The point is that academic papers involving research can be theoretical, conceptual, or practical in nature. For example, a meta-analysis of studies about effective mathematical teaching practices conducted in the last ten years can be written based on the literature and not on empirical data. Yet it is still considered a research paper, and is most likely developed from a research question seeking to explore the effective mathematical practices of elementary teachers (see Figure 3.2).

The most significant part of conducting research is building a clear research question. A research question represents what you want to know about the topic, from your research. Let's take a close look at the role of the research question based on the characteristics of a research paper, which includes a *systemic and in-depth* analysis or *approach* to a topic.

Writing at the graduate level requires illustrating a deep understanding about a particular issue in your paper. This is the most prominent difference between writing about a topic and writing based on a research question. For example, assume you have to write a ten-page paper, and the topic of the paper is your country's school curriculum. You may provide some information about the curriculum such as academic content areas or school days. You may also write about the strengths and weaknesses of the curriculum based on your own experiences. In this case, you may provide general information about the curriculum in your country. In doing so, however, you may fail to offer an in-depth understanding of the curriculum. Also, it may be difficult for you to organize your paper into sections and subsections, because your topic is too broad. If your paper is written without the focus of a research question and just includes information about diverse ideas, the paper may lack an in-depth understanding of the topic in a specific aspect (see Figure 3.3). Although there is diverse information in your paper, your readers may not find meaningful implications. Thus, this type of writing is not appropriate for academic writing. Rather, such "brainstorming" about the topic, as a preliminary writing exercise, may help you develop a research question.

On the other hand, if you write a paper based on a specific research question, you are more likely to express a deep understanding of some aspects of the topic. Assume that you have to answer the following research question: *What is the political meaning of curriculum in my country?* Al-

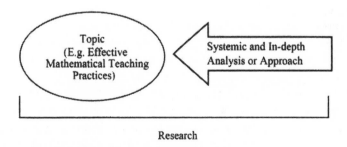

Figure 3.2. The Difference between Topic and Research.

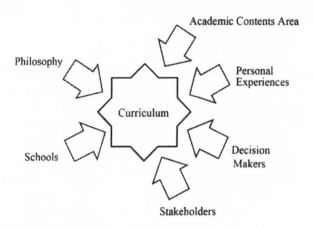

Figure 3.3.   Writing without Research Questions.

though there are several terms and frameworks that should be defined in order to answer the question, you may focus on just one particular aspect of the curriculum in your paper. When writing at the graduate level, you will need to present an in-depth understanding of your subject (see Figure 3.4).

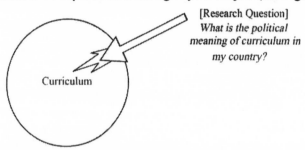

Figure 3.4.   Writing with Research Questions.

In addition, finding the appropriate research question may help you organize the structure of your writing, since you will need to focus on how to answer the research question logically. For example, you may develop the structure of your writing based on the research question (see Figure 3.5).

Figure 3.5 shows an example of an organizing structure for a research paper. But this is not the only approach you can use to organize your paper. While you may develop your own approach, it needs to be organized in a logical way. A detailed explanation about the structure of a research paper will be presented in a subsequent section on "How to Organize Academic Papers."

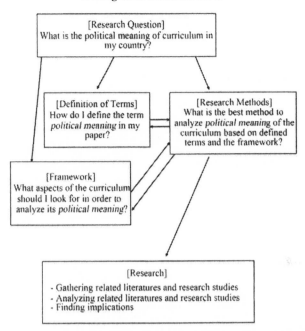

Figure 3.5. Developing the Structure of the Paper Based on the Research Questions.

As noted above, your paper will be more coherent if you develop the appropriate research question and write the paper based on that question (or questions). The appropriate research question may help you frame your topic and develop the research paper.

For all its significance, however, it might not be easy to develop a good research question. It should be neither too broad nor too narrow. For example, the research question, *"What does curriculum look like in South Korea?"* is too broad to answer. On the other hand, the research question, *"Who are the decision-makers for the curriculum in South Korea?"* is too narrow. More precisely, the scope of the research question also varies based on the type of paper; the research question for a ten-page course-work paper will be different from the questions that will guide your dissertation research. In addition, you may consider why your research question is significant to your academic field. Thus, there needs to be practice in order to understand what the appropriate research question is.

If you are still struggling with developing research questions, we recommend getting help from your professors. In some cultures, students believe they should not discuss their work with professors before submitting it to them. In the United States, however, it is acceptable to review your research questions or discuss the overall direction of your paper with your instructors before you start writing. Developing appropriate research questions is part of the coursework you must carry out in learning from your professors. Thus, it is acceptable to discuss your research questions for the paper with them ahead of time.

HOW TO ORGANIZE ACADEMIC PAPERS

Lynn: "The professor told me that my paper was poorly organized. So, I asked him to offer me good examples for academic writing. He said that he couldn't, since there were many ways of organizing academic papers according to the research questions. I don't know what I should do. What was worse, I was not told what was wrong with my paper exactly."

Jeong: "I also have an issue with my writing. I did my best when I wrote the paper and I thought I was following the assignment requirements. However, the professor's feedback was that I failed to present critical viewpoints about the current issue. She said that I just presented information. However, I presented the information with intention. Is my intention the same as my critical viewpoint?"

It is important that you review the assignment and pay close attention to the requirements. If you do not understand what the expectations are, you might consider discussing them with your instructor or with other students. Please keep in mind when developing your paper that you should present your argument in a logical way regarding a specific academic issue or problem. In this case, there are numerous ways of presenting your critical arguments based on research questions, research methods, or frameworks. Thus, it might not be easy to define the appropriate format for academic papers. Although there is no set format, we will discuss some basic components that you might include when writing (see Figure 3.6).

As illustrated in Figure 3.6, we use dashed arrows to represent the sequences of the sections, since the location of the sections might be in a state of flux; some students may locate frameworks under the introduction section, while others may place it in the research method section. Some students may include the literature review in the introduction section, or combine the findings and conclusions sections.

In addition, there might be differences between papers at the master's and doctoral levels regarding the required sections and the scope of them. In general, writings at the master's level may not require students to propose frameworks or research methods. Also, the scope of the literature review might be smaller. Again, as stated earlier in this section, consulting the course syllabus to review the paper's requirements will dictate the approach to the paper. On the other hand, doctoral students' papers may include most of these components except research methods; if the course requires empirical data for your paper, you should present your research methods in your

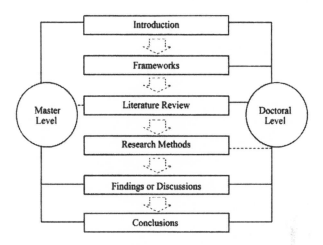

Figure 3.6. The Basic Components for Academic Writings.

paper. Otherwise, you may not need to reveal your research methods. In the latter case, in the introductory section you may briefly illustrate how you organized the data.

Although there might be differences in terms of the required sections, both master's and doctoral students should organize and write papers in an academic manner. To assist you in developing an academic paper, we will briefly discuss each of six suggested components. It is important to note that the suggestions presented are based on our perspective and experience. Thus, we acknowledge that there are other perspectives and approaches.

Introduction

Before you start to write the introduction section of your paper, you should decide on the research questions, your target readers or audience, and the specific academic field. In the previous section, we discussed the significance of the research questions. Similar to the research questions, the target readers or audience play a pivotal role in developing your paper. Context, intent, and language must be appropriate for the target audience. Therefore, these aspects will vary according to the target audiences. For example, your argument and language will be different for policymakers versus researchers; the introduction is written in a way that engages your audience in a topic or problem that is of interest to them. In this case, you may point out current issues in the academic field or critique the deficiency of recent studies' arguments, based on findings from a review of the literature. Additionally, in the introduction section you may present the research question and a brief description of the overall structure of your paper. If needed, you may include the framework of your paper in this section. As noted previously, there are no specific rules for writing papers based on a logical approach toward the research question. In the introductory section, you may clarify what you are going to accomplish in your paper and why your research question is significant.

Although you do not need to identify your target audience in your introduction, it is important to assume familiarity with your readers, because this can help you develop a coherent paper. Another worthy consideration is to note that for some academic papers, the primary audience will be the course instructor. In turn, the instructor may designate experts in your field or your classmates as being the secondary audience or readers. In this case, it will be critical that you adapt the paper regarding tone, argument, and language, so as to meet the expectations of your instructor.

Framework

As discussed in the first chapter, the framework for your paper may provide a lens that demonstrates how the author perceives the major concepts or facts in the paper based on certain theories, philosophies, or practices. When developing the framework for your paper, it should be grounded in viewpoints, concepts, and ideas presented in other studies or conceptual literature. In addition, the framework should support as well as provide insights about the problem or topic that your paper or research will investigate. The following key points might help you when constructing the framework for your paper. Start the introductory section by providing a brief abstract of the key literature; highlight relevant and important concepts or perspectives of the major researchers or writers in the field; discuss how these components relate to your topic or research question; and then place these components in the context of the problem that is the focus of the paper.

Literature Review

According to Pan (2004), "a literature review is a synthesis of the literature on a topic. To create the synthesis, one must first interpret and evaluate individual pieces of literature. Then, the ideas and information they contain must be integrated and restated in order to create a new, original written work." The general purpose of a literature review is to present a current research strand that relates to your topic or research questions. Literature reviews should include your perspective about the topic under discussion, which in turn should include information from relevant studies.

Research Methods

The research method is decided based on a number of elements, such as the research question, topic, problem, or framework. Much will depend on what the course assignment specifies, as well as your intent. Therefore, it is essential that you understand what you are being asked to do and why, which will require careful review of the course syllabus and attention to the professor's directions. In this case, if you do not understand what the expectations are, you must get help from the professor or instructor of the course.

Findings or Discussions

When you read journal articles, you may notice that some researchers use the word *findings*, while others use the term *results,* to describe what the researcher found from the critical analysis of data or relevant literature. There are no specific academic rules for naming this section; researchers usually use *results* for statistical analysis and *findings* for qualitative studies or conceptual papers. It is usually followed by a discussion section, which presents a discussion of the findings or results. For some studies that are qualitative in nature, however, it is not uncommon to have a discussion section that integrates the findings of the study.

Regardless of the approach, the discussion should include both the results of the analysis and your perspective. Thus, to write this section, you will need to apply higher cognitive skills such as analyzing, evaluating, and creating, which we discussed in Chapter One.

Conclusions

You will summarize your findings or results in the conclusion section of your paper. In addition, you may propose some suggestions or implications for your target readers or future researchers.

As noted previously, the titles of each section and their sequence may vary according to how you plan to organize your ideas. You may find that most journal articles include these six sections, although they may use different headings or structures. Thus, when you write a paper at the graduate level, we recommend that you consider these six components. Based on the course requirements and your topic or research questions, you may recreate the structure for the paper with these six components.

APPROPRIATE USE OF CITATIONS

Jenny: "I wrote a paper about the impacts of the law regarding the regulation of air pollution. Every professor I talked with said that the law changed the industry system in the United States. But when I wrote about the impact of the law in my paper, the instructor left a question mark under my statements. I think the professor did not believe my statements because I am an international student."

Solomon: "I cited several articles in order to provide a basis for my statements. However, the professor said that my citations were unreliable. How can I write a paper if the professor does not accept my citations?"

To write a well-documented academic paper, you should present strong arguments based on reliable and valid resources. Among the diverse ways to acquire a robust foundation for your assertions, the most basic rule might be to reference qualified research studies that support your statements. Thus, in this section, we discuss appropriate ways to cite literature or valid sources.

For appropriate citations, you need to check the quality of the literature that you are going to refer to in your paper. In academic fields, there are numerous sources, which are published by diverse academic journals. Unfortunately, there are some journals that may have lower standards than others. Thus, careful attention must be given to the quality of the sources you cite in your paper.

One way to find qualified studies is to use appropriate academic databases when you search for literature related to your topic or research questions. There are academic databases (e.g., *Education Research Complete* or *JSTOR*) that provide qualified articles based on certain criteria. Trying to locate the appropriate database might be a challenge, however, since there are hundreds of them in the academic fields. Thus, the best way to find an appropriate academic database is to ask professors or researchers in your field of study for suggestions. In addition, depending on the topic, problem, or question you are studying, you should consider using more than one qualified academic database. Limiting yourself to just one database may produce a limited number of sources on your topic, leading you to think that these studies are the only sources available. Later, you could be very surprised in reviewing the professor's comments when he lists several other key studies that are relevant to your topic. Your might wonder, "How did I miss these? I searched a reliable database." To avoid such errors, it is best to conduct a more detailed search on your topic or questions by using several databases.

When writing papers, presenting an argument or viewpoint is an important aspect of the work; however, it is equally important to support your argument. Thus, it will be important that you do not outline broad generalizations that are supported by citing a single study. A common mistake graduate students make is having blind faith in published articles. As a member of a community and as scholars, we should respect other researchers' work. At the same time, however, we should try to maintain our own viewpoints. Thus, when you cite other studies in your paper in order to strengthen your arguments, you should cite findings from several studies with similar arguments. You should realize that the findings of a single study might be biased or controversial in academia. Thus, to provide sufficient and proper grounds for your arguments, it is recommended that you use consistent findings from several studies. There are no certain rules regarding the number of references. Yet, as noted above, citing one study to support your argument or perspective might be insufficient. This does not indicate that you need to cite dozens of articles in order to prove that the findings are consistent in a given academic field. Most researchers may cite two to five major studies in order to provide grounds for their statements, unless they need specific research for their framework, research assumptions, or direct quote. The following examples illustrate how this citation might be accomplished. The examples follow the APA style.

- You may develop your argument based on studies that offer similar results. In this case, you may present several studies as illustrated below.

  [Example 1.] Elementary school teachers' knowledge for teaching mathematics is important because teachers at this level are more likely to affect younger students' mathematics achievement than is the case for teachers at the secondary level (Hill, 2008; Konstantopoulos, 2011).

- In order to point out the stream of current research, you may present diverse studies that focus on a similar academic area or share similar scholarly assumptions or perspectives. In this case, you may note that these studies are examples of your arguments by using the abbreviation "e.g.":

  [Example 2.] Diverse approaches have been applied to understand and define elementary teachers' knowledge for teaching mathematics (e.g., Ball, Lubienski & Mewborn, 2001; Bass, 2005; Hill, Ball & Schilling, 2004).

When you choose articles to cite in your paper, you need to confirm the publication year of the articles. It is essential that you are mindful of the period when work or research was published. For example, if a section of your paper presents a historical background for the topic or problem you are studying, it is O.K. to cite articles from that period. However, if your research question or problem relates to current academic issues, refer to studies that were published less than ten years ago.

You should cite what you actually read and understand. When you read an article, you may find that there are several interesting studies from the reference list cited in the article. If you want to cite these studies in your paper, we recommend you find and read the original article. There is a risk in citing other studies without reading them, since there is a possibility that aspects of the study being cited might be a misrepresentation of the original study; sometimes authors focus on only certain parts of a study or rephrase findings inappropriately based on their own understanding.

Appropriate citation is expected for any type of paper that you write; therefore, you should become familiar with the right way to use academic citations. There are several types of citation styles (e.g., APA, American Medical Association, Modern Language Association of America, Chicago Manual of Style, Turabian, or Harvard) but you should apply the style required by the course professor, which is usually specified on the syllabus. If it is not, you should ask the professor which format to use. You should understand that citation styles differ from each other based on the resources (e.g., academic journal, book, or website), and the rules for writing references might vary from one edition to the next. You can check academic citation styles from websites, but we recommend that you buy the latest edition of the manual, if you are planning to continue doing research and writing in the future.

Finally, regardless of what type of paper you are writing, it will be key to your development, as an academic writer, to read many articles and studies within as well as outside your field. When you read, read with a sense of purpose, taking notes on what is relevant to your topic, problem, or question. Then, organize this information for future reference. For example, you may use Excel to make a list of articles or books for future research; you may include information about an article such as the folder where you saved the file, file name, title of an article, authors or published year, and a short summary. This may help you remember the major argument, perspective, or assumption of the article in your future writings.

WRITE IN YOUR OWN WORDS

Hyuk: "For a homework assignment in my statistics class, I had to write the definitions of mean, median, and mode. Thus, I looked up each definition from an online dictionary. I copied and pasted the definition. The next day, the professor e-mailed me and requested that I schedule an appointment to see her. I knew that something was wrong. During the meeting, she showed me the school policy and told me that I had cheated. She said that I was supposed to write each definition in my own words. I couldn't understand what she was talking about. Why am I expected to write definitions in my own words? When I took tests in my country, I had to memorize each definition for a mathematics test. If I did not write them on the test as I had memorized them, I would have gotten those definitions marked wrong on the test."

At all levels of education, you will be required to write papers in your own words. If international students are not familiar with this phrase, it might seem vague, or hard for them to understand. The purpose of writing *in your own words* is to prevent plagiarism. Plagiarism is using or copying the words, thoughts, or ideas of another individual without permission, and then representing the work as your own without giving credit to the original writer. Plagiarism is certainly taken as a serious offense in academic fields. Therefore, one of the clear standards for plagiarism is to use another author's words, ideas, or expressions without citing the original work. This standard extends to figures, pictures, and designs.

Some international students who are not familiar with academic writing plagiarize other researchers' work unintentionally. As shown in Hyuk's case, they may assume that they can use some expressions from the textbook, dictionary, or website, just as they did in high school. However, for an academic paper, you have to apply proper academic citation, even for citing expressions from personal notes posted on a website. In addition, you have to paraphrase what you read, writing *in your own words* and citing the original study to avoid plagiarism. When you paraphrase, use your own words to restate what you have read; the intent is to present the same meaning of the original idea in such a way as to show that you understand it. For example, let's assume that you are going to paraphrase the following statements. You may restate the original articles based on what you understand (see Figure 3.7).

It is not a good idea to paraphrase text by using synonyms as demonstrated (see Figure 3.8). Writing *in your own words* does not merely indicate that you only make simple changes of words in a sentence. Thus, it might be better for you to use a direct quote.

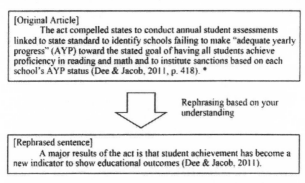

Figure 3.7.   How to Restate the Original Articles.

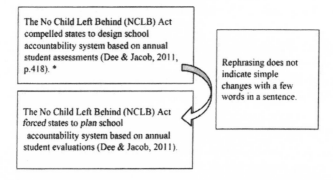

Figure 3.8.   An Example of Improper Ways of Restating the Original Articles.

Another purpose of writing *in your own words* is to broaden academic fields based on diverse approaches. For example, Galileo's heliocentric theory demolished the previously used Ptolemaic system; therefore, any definitions or theories in academic fields can be changed in the future. Thus, it is important for you to understand the topic instead of memorizing it from the textbooks. You may start your own research with these points. This is why most professors require you to explain what you read in your own words, even in a statistics class.

EXTERNAL RULES FOR WRITING

Jan: "There is a professor who is very picky. He even checked my use of words. So, I asked a doctoral student who majored in English literature to check my grammar and word usage in my paper before I submitted it. My friend told me that my paper was O.K. However, the feedback from the professor was that I still needed to improve my writing regarding my selection and use of academics terms. I believe that he underestimated my writing ability because I came from a country where English is not the first language."

Young: "My case is even worse. I got a B+ on a paper, because I did not follow APA style. The professor told me that she loved my ideas. I can't understand why APA style is so important. Maybe . . . she wanted to make some excuses to lower my grade. I feel that she doesn't like me."

As noted at the beginning of this chapter, the external rules of academic papers are as important as the internal rules in writing at the graduate level. No matter how brilliant your ideas are, it might be difficult to deliver them to others if you do not follow the appropriate external rules for academic writing. Also, sophisticated use of words and clear sentences can improve the quality of your academic paper.

In this section, we will discuss some external rules that you should consider when you write academic papers: academic formatting, sophisticated selection of academic language, avoiding long sentences, use of synonyms, and use of direct quotes.

Academic Formatting

As noted in the previous section, there are diverse types of formatting styles for an academic paper. Academic formatting involves rules not only for citations and references but also for ways of presenting data, such as tables or figures. In addition, formatting includes information about how to use punctuation, capitalization, levels of headings, or abbreviations. Although you may not be concerned with publishing the paper you are writing, you need to be familiar with academic formatting as a future researcher. You may get information about academic formatting from websites or publication manuals.

Selection of Academic Language

You may realize that there are differences between the writings of undergraduate and graduate students in terms of their use of language. Thus, the selection of words may affect the quality of your writing. However, you do not need to use difficult words all the time. Rather, you should use appropriate academic language in order to present your ideas clearly.

One way of using appropriate academic language is to refrain from using conversational idiom. There are some expressions that are used mainly in speech but may not be used in formal academic writing. Table 3.1 shows some examples of spoken words and the appropriate expressions in written words (see Table 3.1).

Table 3.1.   Examples of spoken words and the appropriate expressions in written words

Spoken words	Written words
Can, could	May, might
Particularly	In particular
But	However
So	Therefore, thus
Even though	Although

Most U.S. students have learned about the appropriate use of words for academic writing in their middle or high schools. Conversely, it may be difficult for international graduate students who may not have gone to school in the United States to use these terms. Thus, you will need to make the extra effort to develop your academic writing skills in terms of selecting appropriate language for your academic work.

We suggest several ways to improve your writing skills. First, you should pay attention to the authors' use of words when you read academic papers. Published academic papers are good examples of high-quality writing. You can also learn academic expressions or phrases from articles. If you find any good academic words or expressions when you read an article, you may take notes and use them later in your paper. Second, you may ask your professors to provide feedback on your use of words. There are some professors who try to teach academic language to international students by providing feedback on students' written assignments. Unfortunately, there are also some professors who may not understand that international students need extra feedback on their written work. In this case, you may ask the professors for extra feedback via e-mail or by scheduling an appointment during their office hours.

Avoiding Long Sentences

You need to be careful when you use a long sentence in your paper. The intent is not to suggest that long sentences are inappropriate, but that when the academic writing process is very new to you, short sentences are better. Also, with long sentences, there is a greater possibility that you might make grammatical mistakes or use an awkward sentence structure. That way, you may run the risk of confusing the reader and obscuring your meaning. The following example is a long sentence constructed by an international student.

At first, I felt that the professor was giving students a hard time and even trying to be mean, however this behavior helped students think critically, to find the missing points by themselves, they improved their debate skills in the process.

As you see, this student combined three sentences into one. In this case, it would be better to separate them into at least two sentences, as below.

At the beginning, I felt that the professor was rude because he gave students a hard time. Later, I realized that his behavior helped students think critically for themselves, and they were able to improve their debate skills in the process.

Use of Synonyms

Appropriate use of synonyms can improve the quality of your paper. It is recommended that you not use the same word more than once in a sentence or in one paragraph. For example, let's look at the following sentence.

I will assess students' writing skills based on an academic assessment test.

In this case, it would be better to change one word by using a synonym as below.

I will examine students' writing skills based on an academic assessment test.

In order to use synonyms effectively in your writing, you need a wide-ranging vocabulary. You also may get help from a thesaurus on the Internet or from another source. For example, if you want to find a synonym, you can use Microsoft Word by clicking the term that you are looking for (see Figure 3.9).

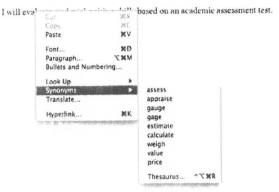

Figure 3.9. How to Find Synonyms in Microsoft Word.

Use of Direct Quotes

There are some students who prefer to use direct quotes in order to prevent plagiarism. Yet overuse of direct quotes may interrupt the smooth flow of the text and make your argument seem vague to the reader. The following paragraph shows an overuse of direct quotes.

> *In chapter three, Burger and Starbird (2012) describe the importance of good questions, suggesting, "Framing good questions focuses your attention on the right issues" (p. 74). To make a good question, one of the most important factors mentioned in this chapter is to find "What's the real question?" (p. 86). The authors suggest that the question must be clarified first. Before asking, "How can I be successful?" (p. 87), it is important to first carefully define the meaning of successful. I personally believe that this process is the most crucial for effective thinking because we should continue to ask questions to better understand a situation or idea.*

Technically, there is no problem with this paragraph. But you may find that you could not concentrate on the content because of the overuse of direct quotes. Also, there are some sentences that do not need a direct quote. You may use direct quotes when the original words have special meaning or when you want to emphasize the author's idea.

In this section, we presented representative cases to illustrate the external rules of writing at the academic level. If you are struggling with these external rules, we recommend that you take a writing course. Your adviser or school counselor may help you find the right course. Also, a good way to improve your writing is to read books about writing skills or vocabularies. Even U.S. students read these types of books in order to improve their writing.

BIBLIOGRAPHY

Ball, D. L., Lubienski, S. T., & Mewborn, D. S. Research on teaching mathematics: The unsolved problem of teachers' mathematical knowledge. In *Handbook of research on teaching* (4th ed., pp. 433–456). Edited by V. Richardson. New York: Macmillan. 2001.

Bass, H. Mathematics, mathematicians and mathematics education. *Bulletin of the American Mathematical Society*, 42(4), 417–430. 2005.

Burger, E. B., & Starbird, M. *The 5 elements of effective thinking*. Princeton, NJ: Princeton University Press. 2012.

Dee, T. S., & Jacob, B. The impact of No Child Left Behind on student achievement. *Journal of Policy Analysis and Management, Vol. 30*, 418. 2011.

Hill, H. C. Mathematical knowledge for teaching and the mathematical quality of instruction: An exploratory study. *Cognition and Instruction*, 430–511. 2008.

Hill, H. C., Ball, D. L & Schilling, S. G. Developing measures of teachers' mathematics knowledge for teaching. *Elementary School Journal*, 105, 11–30. 2004.

Konstantopoulos, S. Teacher effects in early grades: Evidence from a randomized study. *Teachers College Record*, 113. 2011.

Pan, M. *Preparing literature reviews: qualitative and quantitative approaches.* Glendale, CA: Pryczak Publishing. 1. 2004.

Chapter Four

Preparing Classroom Presentations

INTRODUCTION

There are two types of classroom presentations: an individual presentation and a group presentation. While an individual presentation mainly focuses on effective delivery of a personal study, a group presentation may emphasize providing in-depth understanding of a certain topic based on the interactions among group members.

Although most international students have had experience with academic presentations as undergraduate students in their own country, they may feel concerned about giving a presentation in a graduate course because they will need to speak their second language. Thus, presenting a topic in English will require a major effort.

In this chapter, we describe ways of preparing and leading presentations in class. This chapter will provide general guidance for classroom presentations rather than focusing on specific types of presentations. Covering the different types of presentations, based on the topics, purpose, or characteristics of the academic area, is beyond the scope of this book.

PRACTICING FOR ORAL PRESENTATIONS

Ki: "I messed up my presentation. I can speak well in Korean, but it is hard for me to recall appropriate English words while thinking about the content that I must deliver during the presentation. Even worse, I became nervous during my presentation, I started to talk very fast. I also knew that my pronunciations were not good. I felt that no one in the class understood what I was saying."

Jen: "I had a similar experience. So, I decided to read my notes during my presentation. However, I got a B+ for my presentation. The professor told me that I received a low grade because I just read my notes to the class during the presentation."

For international students whose first language is not English, giving a presentation in front of the class might be a frightening experience. Also, there are some languages that have a different syntax from English; the location of verbs and objects is reversed and the use of articles is different. Thus, it makes sense that international students do not speak as fluently as U.S. students when giving a presentation. Also, international students may become nervous when they give a speech in front of U.S. students. Unfortunately, in terms of a classroom presentation, using the fact that your first language is not English may not be an excuse. Regardless of your speaking ability, the professor or instructor assesses your presentation using the same criteria they use to assess U.S. students. Thus, taking time to practice your speech will help you give a better presentation; this is not only for a good grade but also to practice what you plan to say to the class, which will make the information you prepared clear to them.

Acknowledging that giving class presentations might be difficult for some international students, we present two strategies that might assist you in providing effective presentations.

The first step for preparing a presentation is to make notes for your speech. It might not be easy to memorize what you want to say during the presentation in English. Preparing notes to assist you during a presentation is not a new idea. For example, most of the U.S. presidents have read prepared notes for their public speeches. Another example is newscasters who read scripts when they report news on TV. The key is that your speech should not sound like you are reading but as if you are speaking. To make your speech sound like you are speaking, there are several things you need to consider when you make notes for a presentation.

If You Are Going to Use a Presentation Program Such as PowerPoint or Prezi, Do Not Write Information in Your Notes That Will Be Listed on Your Presentation Slide

One of the purposes of a presentation is to engage your audience in the topic by presenting it in an interesting and/or creative way. Thus, when necessary, you should explain the concept or idea so as to offer insight, rather than just presenting factual information about the topic. Thus, you have to focus on how to explain the concepts rather than simply reading the information on your presentation slides.

Write Your Notes Using Simple Words and Sentences

You should understand that there are some differences between words used for writing and for speaking. When you read academic journals, you may notice that the words and sentence structures are different from what might be used in everyday conversation. Thus, when you make notes for the presentation, you should keep in mind what you are going to say. When you make notes for your presentation, you may not want to use academic words that are unfamiliar or hard to pronounce. If you use unfamiliar words or poor sentence structures, your audience may become disengaged because they do not understand what you are saying. Therefore, it is suggested that you make use of synonyms with similar meanings that you can pronounce with ease.

The second step is to practice. Although you may consider some words and sentences simple when you make notes, they may sound strange when you actually say them. You may need to rewrite some parts of your notes so that you are comfortable saying them. Also, you need to work on your pronunciation, intonation, and volume. Although it might be difficult practicing by yourself, you should certainly do it. You may ask your U.S. friends to check your speech. If you are uncomfortable asking U.S. friends, then you may get help from electronic devices. For example, you may check pronunciation and accents by using Google Translator (http://translate.google.com/). If you input the sentences in the translator and click the speaker icon, the program reads them in English for you (see Figure 4.1). It is important to note that the Google translator might present translations that are inaccurate grammatically.

You may record your own voice with this program. You do not need to practice all the sentences that you are going to read, because it is time consuming. You should practice the key sentences or words that are difficult for you to pronounce.

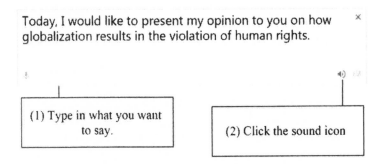

Figure 4.1.   Practice Your Pronunciation with Google Translator.

Although you may work hard on preparing presentations, you should understand that not all of them will be successful. The key is that you should never give up; you need time to become familiar with public speaking in English. Also, you should remember that your English-speaking competency does not represent your intellect. You need to do your best all the time.

LEARN HOW TO WORK WITH YOUR GROUP MEMBERS

Yoon: "I said to the professor I wanted to present alone instead of with a group."

Alejandro: "Why did you want to present without a group? You are an international student. You may get some help from your group members."

Yoon: "I know, but I felt sorry for my group members. Last semester, my group presentation was a disaster. My group members did almost everything. Even when they discussed the presentation, I was not able to participate because I was afraid to speak English, and I lack confidence. Also, I did not know much about the presentation style required. So, I felt like I became an invisible man when we had a meeting. It was an embarrassing experience for me. Although I may receive a low grade on my presentation, I feel more comfortable when I present alone."

Most U.S. students are kind to international students. You should understand, however, that there are some students who do not want to work with international students. A U.S. student explained why she did not want to work with international students:

A U.S student: "I prefer not to be on a team with international students. They do not provide any ideas during the discussion when we prepare for the presentation. Also, they always make excuses. They always say that their speech is not good and that they are not familiar with U.S. classrooms. They are too passive. What is worse, although they do not work hard, they usually receive the same grade I do."

This is only one person's perspective based on her experience or perception. There is always another perspective. For example, an international student shared his experience about group presentations:

An international student: "I had to prepare a presentation with a group. In my group, there was a girl who was so mean. She ignored me and always tried to talk only with the other U.S. students. She did not look at me when she was talking. When I tried to say something, she said that it was not a good idea. I was embarrassed and felt humiliated."

These excerpts show the difficulties experienced by international students when working in groups. Due to these reasons, some international students prefer to work alone, or to work in groups that consist only of other international students.

If you avoid working with U.S. students, however, you may also lose opportunities to let your U.S. peers learn something from you. In addition, you may not learn how to work with the U.S. students. In the United States, you can learn not only from the professors but also from the students: how they approach the topic, how they prepare presentations, and how they reconcile different ideas. These experiences will be helpful when you work with diverse people in society.

In order to learn something from the U.S. students and to let them know what you know, you should focus on what you can and cannot do. Also, you should be honest and trust your group members. The following case shows how you might build rapport with your group members.

> *An international student: "When I first met my group members, I knew that they did not like me. They looked disappointed. During the discussion, they just talked to each other. I didn't blame them. If I were them, I would not want to work with international students with speech issues, but I knew that I should do something. So I told them about what I could do for our group and what I needed from the group. I said that I could make the presentation slides and search for data. So, I took on the responsibility of making the presentation slides. But I needed some help with the oral communication part. I knew that I would need help during the question and answer part of the presentation; so, I asked them to help me if I was not able to provide a clear answer in English. We divided our work fairly. I did my best to finish my job. Our presentation was good, and we received a grade of A. My team tried to help me, and I also tried to help them. Next semester, by chance, we took the same course. Surprisingly, they came to me first, stating that they wanted to work with me for the group presentation. Thus, I gained more by being proactive. If I had been a passive member and allowed the other group members to do all the work, there is a strong possibility that the results may have been different, and they would not have approached me to work with them in the next course we took together."*

The episode shows that you may need to be humble when you work in a group. The international student in the episode let the group members know what she could and could not do, and asked them for help. At the same time, she tried to contribute something to the presentation. She had an open mind and did her best. As a result, she learned something from the U.S. students and vice versa.

During graduate studies, you are able to improve your academic knowledge; however, it is during this time that you also develop your social skills. There are future scholars who have diverse backgrounds in your university.

Learning how to work effectively with these future scholars will help you in your academic field in the years to come.

INVOLVE YOUR AUDIENCE IN THE PRESENTATION

Ken: "When I listened to international students give a presentation, it was boring, and sometimes I couldn't understand what they were saying, although I am an international student, too. I don't want my presentation to be boring. I want my audience to become involved in my presentation. But, at the same time, I'm afraid that I may not appropriately answer the questions asked by the audience. I know that just displaying information during the presentation might be boring to the audience. However, I am afraid to communicate with my classmates during the presentation because of my English ability."

Yaoming: "I had to prepare a 20-minute presentation on a certain topic. During the presentation, I just read my notes. I was too nervous at that time, so I read fast. I just finished reading my notes in ten minutes and finished my presentation. I saw that the professor was concerned, since my presentation should have been 20 minutes."

There are many advantages to involving your audience during your presentation. You can check their understanding of the information, and provide more explanation based on their comprehension. In addition, engaging your audience will help them listen to your explanation attentively. At the same time, you can manage your presentation by allowing a few minutes for discussion, and expanding the question-and-answer session if you finish ahead of time.

Engaging the audience by asking questions and responding to their questions is not easy for international students whose oral English speech is not sufficient to lead discussions. Some international students may feel burdened by involving the audience because they believe that they may not be capable of answering all the questions. It is important to remember that you do not need to explain everything. You may communicate with your audience during the presentation by using some of the strategies given below.

Use Specific Questions

A lot of presenters often use the question, *"Do you have any questions so far?"* In the classroom, the professors and the U.S. students also use this question during or after their presentations. This is a good leading question to present to your audience. But some international students are afraid to use this question because they worry that they may not understand how to answer the questions asked by the audience in response.

We know that this is not a matter of international students' understanding of the topic. Rather, it is about their limited vocabulary and experience with presentations. In this case, we recommend you use a specific question rather than broad ones. For example, if you have a certain topic that you want your audience to focus on, some good questions might be: *"What do you think about the topic?" "Do you agree or disagree?"* or, *"Do you have any experiences related to the topic?"* Using these questions will help the audience focus on the topic that you are familiar with or want to discuss. Also, your audience may feel that they are engaging in the presentation.

Let Your Audience Answer the Question

Although you may use specific questions during the presentation, you might want to use a broad question at the end of the presentation in order to check your audience's understanding and to find missing parts in your presentation. You do not need to be worried about asking, *"Do you have any questions so far?"* If you cannot understand the questions from the U.S. students, you may ask them to *please repeat the question.* If you still do not understand the question or do not know the answer, you may get help from your audience. You may ask your audience, *"Is there anyone who wants to answer the question?"* If there is no one who wants to answer, you may point out one student in your audience. It does not matter whether the student's answer is good or bad. You may get some clues from the student's answer or gain some time to think about your own answers.

Provide Some Ideas as to What You Want to Talk About

At the beginning of your presentation, a good strategy is to provide clues about the topic of discussion; the clues may help your audience stay focused on the topic during the presentation. At the end of the presentation, you may discuss the major points with your audience comfortably, since you already know what your audience is going to talk about.

For example, you might conduct a short survey about a certain topic at the beginning of your presentation. You would provide the audience with a Post-it note to write their opinion about whether they agree with the survey question or not. They would then post the note on the chalkboard (see Figure 4.2).

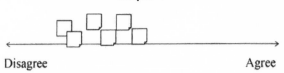

Disagree   Agree

Figure 4.2.   An Example of Encouraging Audience Involvement in Your Presentation (1).

At the end of your presentation, you could conduct a second survey in the same way (see Figure 4.3). Some of the students in your audience may have changed their opinions, but some of them may not. But this does not matter to you. You may ask your audience about the survey results and support them as they discuss their ideas.

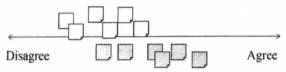

Disagree   Agree

Figure 4.3.   An Example of Encouraging Audience Involvement in Your Presentation (2).

You may develop diverse activities based on your topic. The key is to set the range of the topic your audience may focus on during your presentation. It will lead your audience to think about the topic deeply during the presentation. Also, it will be helpful for you because you may be able to anticipate your audience's reaction, and prepare vocabularies and examples to be used during the discussion or Q & A time.

In order to use these strategies, you should prepare the presentation carefully. Moreover, you should try not to panic during the presentation. As noted previously, it may not be easy to talk in a second language in public. You have to believe in yourself and have confidence in your ability as well.

Chapter Five

Developing Social and Academic Relationships

INTRODUCTION

Studying in English at the graduate level is not the only difficulty that international students may encounter. Some international students struggle in their social relationships with professors or other students due to cultural differences. In this section, we will discuss some etiquette in the academic field, in order to help international students build good relationships with the graduate school community.

ACADEMIC RELATIONSHIPS WITH PROFESSORS

Naomi: "When the course started, I realized that the amount of reading was too heavy for me. I needed extra time, because English is not my first language. Thus, I decided to talk with the professor. Before I came to the United States, I had heard that U.S. professors are kind and are willing to help international students. When I met the professor, I told him that the amount of reading was too burdensome for me. I expected some words of encouragement, but he said, 'U.S. students also are struggling with studying. If you cannot handle it, you should leave the program.' I was shocked and embarrassed by his response."

Rosa: "I had a similar experience. I had a simple question regarding the course syllabus. I went to the professor's office, and the door was opened. So, I entered the room. When the professor saw me, she seemed upset. She

*said that I should e-mail her before visiting her office. She asked me to
leave the room."*

Developing relationships with professors is important because it can
make or break your studies in the United States. As discussed in previous
chapters, you can improve your writing or speaking by getting help from
your professors. If you do not learn these academic skills from your professors, it may be hard for you to become a scholar in your academic field.

In order to build good relationships with your professors, there are several
things to consider. You may have heard that most U.S. professors are willing
to help students. This is true. However, this does not indicate that they will
do everything for you. You should understand that there are limits regarding
what you may ask and what you should not ask them. Also, if you do not
know how to get help from them, you may not be able to obtain what you
need. In this section, we will provide some tips that might assist you in
developing effective relationships with professors.

What You Can Ask, and What You Should Not Ask

When you join a graduate program in the United States, you are expected to
study and perform similar to the U.S. students. If you cannot follow the
coursework due to lack of English ability, you should not have applied for
graduate study at a U.S. university. Thus, you should not ask your professors
to reduce the amount of required readings or to provide extra help when you
are developing a classroom presentation. In the same vein, you should not
say that you do not want to participate in a classroom discussion because
your speech in English is not good. Such an announcement may sound like
whining.

On the other hand, during class, you may ask questions about what you do
not understand. Also, during a scheduled appointment with the professor,
you may give suggestions about the kind of feedback that you need for your
coursework. For example, before you submit a paper, you may gently request
them to provide extra feedback on your use of academic terms. You may ask
for feedback on your speech, during discussion, as well as your plan for your
classroom presentation. You should realize that professors and instructors do
not have to accept your request for feedback. Thus, you should ask them in a
very polite way. Rather than saying "*I want your feedback on my use of
words in my paper,*" you may ask, "*Could you please help me improve my
writing? There are some academic terms that I cannot find in my dictionary.
So, I hope you can provide some feedback on my use of academic terms.*"
Remember, you may ask for help from your professors in order to achieve
the objectives of the course.

Get Help from the Teaching Assistants

Some professors will allow their graduate assistants to help students with understanding various course assignments and activities. In this case, professors will announce at the beginning of the semester that this is one of the roles of the graduate assistants. These professors might include the graduate assistant's contact information on the syllabus. For example, you may be able to e-mail the graduate assistant when you have questions about coursework or papers. If a graduate assistant is available, do not hesitate when you need help. You must be a proactive student and not a passive one.

Visit Your Professors during Their Office Hours

If you need to speak with your professors, it is recommended that you visit them during their office hours. Office hours indicate the time that the professor has set up for student advising. Usually, professors post their office hours on their syllabus, and in some cases, on their office door. But this does not indicate that you may visit their office without making an advance arrangement. There are possibilities that several students might want to go to the office at the same time or that the professor may have an unexpected meeting. Thus, we recommend making an appointment before you visit the office; you may request a meeting with your professor via e-mail. If the office hours do not work for you, you may also ask them to schedule a meeting for another time. To ensure that you are able to meet with the professor, make sure you follow whatever guidelines are listed in the course syllabus or announced by the professor at the beginning of the course.

Ask for an Extension If You Need It

In some countries, no excuses will be allowed for late submission of an assignment. At many U.S. universities, however, it is not uncommon for students to ask for an extension for an assignment, provided they have a valid reason (e.g., serious illness or a family emergency). But the definition of "a valid reason" might differ depending on the professor. It is important to note that although this might be the practice, some professors will not accept late assignments for any reason. If a situation occurs that warrants an extension for an assignment, you might consider checking with the graduate assistant to see if your reason is valid. Furthermore, when you ask for an extension, you should request permission at least a couple of days before the due date via e-mail. An occasional request is acceptable, because we cannot control unexpected incidents. Thus, it is essential that you do not make a habit of asking for extensions. Plan ahead and make every effort to stay on top of your coursework.

Use E-mail

While in some cultures it is considered impolite to make requests by e-mail, U.S. professors may prefer using e-mail to your coming in person or calling them on the phone. All e-mail communications in which you address the professor, instructor, or graduate assistant must be phrased in a professional and formal way. Although a professor or graduate assistant may have asked you to address them by their first name, when you e-mail them, it is important to use their title and last name (e.g., Professor Smith, Dr. Hall, or Ms. King, instead of "Hey Professor"). The aim is not to be sloppy; you should try to follow a standard writing protocol that includes correct spelling, grammar, and punctuation rules. Another element to consider is keeping your message short and to the point. The overall goal is to be brief, concise, and clear. Clarity in the appropriate use of e-mail includes listing the course number and name as well as the purpose of your message in the subject heading. Finally, never start a message with, "I would like to ask you a favor" or "I need you to do me a favor." If you are communicating with a friend, then asking for a favor is all right, but professors do not do favors for students.

You need to realize that you are the one who needs help. This does not mean that you must eat humble pie all the time, however. You should find a way to stand up for your rights as a student in a polite way. Some international students may say that they want to be polite, but they cannot because of cultural differences. You may not know some of the rules of etiquette in the United States; however, you should understand that if you approach them in a polite way and with sincerity, the professors will know it and respect you in the same way.

PERSONAL RELATIONSHIPS WITH PROFESSORS

Michiko: "I heard that it is O.K. to use a professor's first name in the United States. So, when I met my adviser, I called her by her first name. The professor told me that I should call her by her last name because we were not friends. I was embarrassed because I felt like I had made a mistake."

Chen: "I bought a small Christmas gift for a professor who teaches one of my courses. In our country, it is O.K. to give gifts to professors. Also, I believe that we have a good relationship. I wanted to thank him. I expected him to be happy with my gift, but he became upset when he saw it. He said that he couldn't take it and asked me to leave his office."

As you find more opportunities to talk with professors during the semester, you may become close to them. But you should also realize that you might ruin the relationship if you do not respect U.S. academic culture. As shown in the cases of Michiko and Chen, your action might be considered rude, even though it was unintentional. Also, you should try to learn the etiquette of the academic field. Here are several things that you should consider regarding etiquette in personal meeting with professors.

Do Not Call Your Professor by Their First Name without Their Permission

When you start your graduate program, you may notice that some U.S. students call professors by their first names. Thus, you might think that it is O.K. for you to call them by their first name as well. Still, you should know that some professors prefer that students not address them by their first names. Moreover, it is considered rude to address professors by their first names without permission. For this reason, it is recommended that you use their last names until you have permission to use their first names. For example, if the professor's name is John Smith, you may address him as Dr. Smith or Professor Smith. If the professor wants you to use his first name, he may say, "Please call me John." After that, you can call him John, because he has given you permission.

Do Not Give Any Gifts to Your Professors during the Semester

We highly discourage you from giving gifts to professors while you are enrolled in their classes, because the professor may view this act negatively. Thus, your gifts may put your professors in a difficult position. If you want to thank them for their help, you may send them a card during the holiday season. Also, you may give them small souvenirs from your own country after the course is over.

Respect Their Time

Professors are very busy with commitments beyond teaching and research. Therefore, it is important that you respect their time. If you cannot attend a scheduled meeting, you should let your professor know as early as possible. You should also avoid showing up at their office without notification. However, there may be times when a problem emerges, and you need to see the professor immediately. First, contact them by e-mail, informing them of the situation. Then, make a request for an appointment. Second, if you are not able to schedule an appointment via e-mail, you may go to the office and ask politely if you can talk with them for a few minutes. When you are given permission, you should state your case and be as brief and concise as possible.

You do not need to be nervous when you meet with your professors. Although they assess your coursework, they will not evaluate personal conversations. Also, some international students say "I'm sorry" repeatedly, when they do not understand the conversation; based on some students' cultural traditions, it is appropriate to say this. You may say it once or twice during the conversation, but you do not need to say it repeatedly. One of the reasons you chose to study in the United States was to improve both your academic knowledge and your English. Thus, you do not need to be sorry for your English level or academic skills. All you need to do is to work hard in order to learn as much as you can. If you cannot follow the conversation, you may ask your professor, "Will you please say that again?" or "You are saying . . . ?" When you are new to America, it is not necessary for you to apologize for not understanding U.S. culture or idioms. But while these strategies will work for you initially, when you have been in the United States for several years, being sorry for making careless mistakes will not work. The goal is to show continuous improvement in your academic studies.

RELATIONSHIPS WITH OTHER STUDENTS

TaeHyun: "I'm looking for a roommate. I hope that my roommate is the same nationality as I am. We can share our food and also have conversations in our first language. It would be good for me."

Juno: "I never go to the Korean Students Association, although I came from South Korea. I came here to study English. I feel it is a waste of time to hang out with Korean students in the United States. I'll just try to make some American friends."

Some international students prefer to socialize with students who are from similar cultural backgrounds, while others prefer to socialize with American students. While there is no correct answer to this, we recommend that you try to meet diverse people, including Americans and students from other countries. When you interact and work with diverse friends, there are several things you need to consider.

Do Not Discuss Your Future Research

Graduate students are potentially future scholars. Thus, there is a possibility that their ideas from their coursework may lead to future research. You should be careful when you discuss your ideas with your friends because it might be difficult to claim copyright later. You may ask some questions in order to develop your ideas, but you do not need to describe every detail of your ideas to your friends.

Be Careful When You Share Your Ideas or Work

All universities have policies regarding academic integrity. A major aspect of these policies includes universities supporting as well as encouraging graduate students to share their ideas with their peers, but also strongly advocating that students take responsibility and get credit for their work. Therefore, as an international student, you might want to share your papers and other written assignments with your peers. If you decide to do this, then you must be careful, ensuring that your peers do not copy your ideas or the paper itself. A good rule to follow is to not share your work with someone who is enrolled in the same course as you.

Respect Other Students' Cultures and Backgrounds

Life as an international student will present many challenges and potential adversities. Thus, you may feel relaxed when you talk with students in your native language because you do not need to try too hard to impress them with your intelligence, although they might have a different academic background. Also, it is a good idea to participate in a student association or organization, such as the International Korean Students Association.

Sometimes, students from different cultures or countries might say that your culture is weird. They may think this because they are not familiar with your culture traditions or norms. The best you might do is to respect cultural differences with the hope that your culture will be respected as well. Also, interacting with students from diverse cultures might provide you with the opportunity to learn about them, and for you to share your culture with them. It may be easier to only interact with students with similar cultural backgrounds; however, this is counter to why you came to the United States. If you only want to interact or socialize with students from your culture, then ask yourself, "Why did I choose to study in America?"

In summary, one of the merits of studying in America is that there are many international students who come from all over the world, as well as from different regions of the United States. You can be a friend with someone who comes from Africa, Asia, Europe, Alaska, or Puerto Rico. It is a great chance for you to broaden your world perspective. You may learn about their cultural traditions and languages. Also, you may learn how to work closely with diverse students. It may be uncomfortable or difficult for some international students who have an introverted personality, but you should at least try.

86811218R00048

Made in the USA
Columbia, SC
06 January 2018